Labanotation

by

Ann Hutchinson

President of the

DANCE NOTATION BUREAU, INC.

Illustrated by Doug Anderson

THEATRE ARTS BOOKS
New York

Library of Congress Catalog Card No. 61-9872

First published by Theatre Arts Books in 1966
under arrangement with New Directions,   the
original publishers, the author, and the Dance
Notation Bureau, Inc.

ACKNOWLEDGEMENTS

The work of preparing this book was aided
by a grant from the Rockefeller Foundation.

The organization of the material in this book
was accomplished through the assistance
of Selma Jeanne Cohen.

The autography of the Labanotation examples and
studies by Marian van Loen.

Reference materials have included Albrecht Knust's books,
"Abriss der Kinetographie Laban" (Handbook of Kinetography) and "Handbuch der Kinetographie Laban" (Dic-
tionary of Kinetography). Figs. 468-71 in the
chapter on group notation are based on
examples devised by Mr. Knust.

Printed in the United States of America

Published by THEATRE ARTS BOOKS
333 Sixth Avenue, New York 10014

Labanotation

DEDICATION

To Laban
for being a genius

To my first dance and notation
teachers for putting up with me

To my husband for putting up with notation

To the advisors of the Dance Notation Bureau
for their constant encouragement

To the many members of the Bureau who have contributed so much to the growth of Labanotation in
general and to the work of this
book in particular

PREFACE

by George Balanchine

The subject of dance notation has interested me since I first encountered it as a student at the Imperial Dancing Academy in Russia.
At that time I studied the Stepanov method, a system based exclu-
sively on the classic ballet vocabulary and unsuited for the recording
of any other kind of dance. In spite of its limitations, knowledge of
it made me aware of what was needed in a sound system of movement notation. Later, as a choreographer, I became more sharply
aware of the need for an accurate and workable method for notating
my works. To me, the prime requisite of such a notation system
would be its ability to correlate faithfully the time values in the
dance with the music, because my choreography either closely follows the line of the music or contrasts directly with it.

When I heard of Laban's system of notation it seemed the most
completely developed method evolved to meet this need. After
studying the system and watching Ann Hutchinson, America's leading notator and teacher at work, I realized that this was indeed the
answer and I decided to embark immediately on the long-range pro-
ject of having my ballets recorded. "Symphony in C, " "Orpheus, "
"Theme and Variations, " "Symphonie Concertante, " and "Bourrée
Fantasque" are among those already completed. Thanks to these
scores I am now assured that these ballets will be accurately performed in the future.

As the musician needs to record the precise and minute details
of his composition to insure correct performance of his score, so
the choreographer needs a notation capable of equal accuracy. While
some people advocate the use of films to record ballet, I have found

them useful only in indicating the style of the finished product and in suggesting the general over-all visual picture and staging. A film cannot reproduce a dance step by step, since the lens shoots from but one angle and there is a general confusion of blurred impressions which even constant re-showing can never eliminate. Labanotation records the structure of a dance, revealing with perfect clarity each of the specific movements of each performer.

Through Labanotation we can actually sit down and compare or analyze different styles of dance. Even the complicated techniques and studies take up little space and are easy to reconstruct intellectually through the notated patterns. There is no longer any need to wade through pages of verbal descriptions, which eventually become unintelligible.

In making the grant to Miss Hutchinson for the preparation of this book, the Rockefeller Foundation demonstrated its belief in the value of this system of notation and in the influence which its widespread use will have on the future development of dance. I am grateful for this belief and for the creative policy of this humanistic fund, for I am one of the choreographers who will benefit from the increased acceptance and use of Labanotation. I believe that it will soon be universally recognized as being as necessary to the dancer as musical notation is to the musician. Ann Hutchinson is the ideal person to have prepared this definitive text book, which will be of inestimable value to all persons working in the field of dance.

New York
April, 1954

FOREWORD

by Rudolf Laban

Approximately two hundred years ago a writer on the manners and morals of the French court, J. P. Menetrier, complained that on the night tables of the ladies one could find many more choreographies than Bibles. It has to be surmised that these ladies were able to read the choreographies of dances written in the famous Beauchamps-Feuillet dance notation.* We assume that they could read them as fluently as music notation or ordinary writing, which were all subjects of their general education.

During the last fifty years an increasing number of people have had a nodding acquaintance with dance notation, and some are even convinced that written dance, or script-dance, is a cultural necessity of our time.

The author of this book, Ann Hutchinson, has for more than ten years contributed in a most efficient way to the spreading of script-dance in the United States. Miss Hutchinson and her numerous associates call this system of movement notation "Labanotation," in which title my own name is incorporated. I am most honoured, not only by this fact but also by her request that I write a few introductory words to her book.

In my early publications on this subject I have always stressed the point that the endeavour to describe the movements of a dance in special symbols has one main purpose. That is the creation of a

---

*Beauchamps was recognised in 1666 by a French Act of Parliament as the inventor of a system of dance notation. Feuillet published dances recorded in this notation a few decades later.

literature of movement and dance. It is obvious that notation or script facilitates the communication of movement ideas to other people. When, ages ago, mankind awoke to the idea of standardising pictures and signs in order to communicate certain ideas to one another, bodily actions and gestures were of course included from the very beginning. Early forms of writing are full of signs or symbols for action and movement. No form of writing could possibly omit the enormous number of verbs which, to a great extent, are always bodily actions involving movement. In my search for primary action signs, I found fascinating examples of movement description in the mantic symbols invented by ancient Tibetan monks and in the cuneiform characters of the Assyrians and Babylonians. In Egyptian and Chinese scripts I found a rich variety of movement symbols which are, in a sense, the archetypes of dance notation signs.

Noverre, the creator of the "Ballet d'Action," in which the rigid steps of his predecessors were liberated into a rich and all-round expression of the whole body, was a decided enemy of dance notation. He preferred to record the contents of his ballets in words. This is most regrettable for us because we have great difficulty in reconstructing his famous movement inventions from the contemporary drawings and illustrations of his productions. The dances written down by Feuillet do not need to be reconstructed, they can be simply read by anyone who takes the trouble to learn his system of notation.

In my recent book* on this subject I took the functional movement order on which Feuillet's notation is based as granted. His basic principles are universally valid and his system of notation is simple and rational - the egg of Columbus, as it were. One wonders that they were not discovered much earlier.

The first problem that faced modern notators of dance was to overcome the prejudice that a choreographic script is unable to describe all the subtle variations of movement in modern stage dancing and indeed in all other kinds of dance styles. Ballet, modern dance, folk and national dances, including all the historic and exotic forms of dancing which we study and perform today, cannot, it is true, be precisely fixed with Feuillet's restricted symbols, so the

*"Principles of Dance and Movement Notation," by Rudolf Laban (Macdonald & Evans, London).

modern notator had to create a form of movement notation which would be able to serve the purposes of industrial operations, of educational exercise and of psychological movement investigation.

So far as my own research is concerned, years of struggle were filled with the study of ancient movement symbols, with experiment and with controversial discussions. In the early twenties I decided to write two volumes containing the details of my investigations.[*] Only one volume appeared. Instead of the second volume, I compiled, a few years later, the first edition of the "Method and Orthography of Kinetography Laban. "

Much has happened in the twenty-five years since the formulation of a contemporary dance-script became possible. The advent of a new generation of movement notators has made it possible to try out my ideas on a larger scale. My late friend and colleague, Dussia Bereska, who some forty years ago was the only supporter of my notation ideas and of my hope for a future script-dance literature, predicted the coming development with astonishing accuracy. To her are due my greatest thanks for the encouragement and advice which accompanied me on the thorny path of the first consolidation of the system.

In later years a number of enthusiastic supporters have helped to improve my first conception. A system of notation cannot arise from the solitary endeavour of one person only. The great merits of our senior dance notator, Albrecht Knust, are well-known, but people who have excelled chiefly in other fields of the dance as Kurt Jooss, Sigurd Leeder, Lisa Ullmann and others - have also contributed much to the early development of our system.

I have often been sceptical because I believed that it would be several generations before the creation of a dance literature could become a reality. However, we have moved on more quickly and here now, in 1955, is this book of Ann Hutchinson as a harbinger of things to come. Her activity as the founder and leader of the New York Dance Notation Bureau has everywhere awakened keen interest and appreciation. I can say that the gratitude of all people striving for the creation of a literature of dance and movement, with its own

*"Choreographie" - First Volume, Publishers: Diedericks Jena, 1926.

language and its own symbolic representation, is secured for this young author.

We must remember, too, that much has been collected and much is waiting to be published in the Dance Notation Bureau's desk and in many other places. A script-dance literature actually exists, if only in manuscript.

What do we expect to find in the script-dance libraries of the future? We surely need technical works on the orthography and proper use of the system. Training manuals are needed to develop capable notators. There must be books useful for spreading knowledge of movement and dance through the curricula of schools. Material on movement notations in industry and therapy, which younger notators have already begun to collect and record, will also have its place in future libraries and will indicate the possible ties for scientific research in many fields, such as anthropology where the symbols of early times could be transcribed into the new idiom of modern dance notation.

The manifestation of human spirituality which has made dance a sister art of poetry and music can survive only if its products are written, printed and read by a large circle of laymen and performers. One could go on to describe what has to be done and what is partly already there, but unfortunately out of reach of the great public, such as a veritable encyclopaedia in many volumes by Albrecht Knust, in which all the possible variants of human movement are recorded. What the author of this present book, Ann Hutchinson, has already done in the field merits appreciation exceeding the limits of this foreword. I can only say that I heartily welcome this publication as an early flower in a fertile soil, where the productive spirit of our young dance creators and notators, I sincerely trust, will be able to plant solid roots.

Studio Lodge
Addlestone, Surrey

Table of Contents

A Brief History of Dance Notation   1

Introduction to Labanotation   5

Chapter

I   Fundamentals of Labanotation   9

II   Steps and Arm Movements   23

III   Variations in Steps and Arm Gestures, Positions of the Feet   36

IV   Jumps, Open Positions of the Feet   51

V   Leg Gestures, Flexing and Stretching   66

VI   Circular Path, Turns, Use of Body and Space Holds   81

VII   Floor Plans, Drafting a Score, Repeat Signs   97

VIII   Touch, Slide, Brush   115

IX   The Parts of the Limbs   130

X   Passive Movements, Uses of the Body   145

PART TWO

Chapter

XI   Subtleties of Movement   167

XII   Kneeling, Sitting, Lying   190

XIII   Rotations of the Limbs   202

XIV   Rotations of the Body   213

XV   Revolutions of the Body   221

XVI   Deviations   232

XVII   Part Leading, Successions   238

XVIII   Details of Body Areas   246

XIX   Group Notation   251

XX   Effort   257

        Alphabet of Basic Symbols   263

        Glossary of Supplementary Symbols   266

        Index   269

A Brief History of Dance Notation

For at least five centuries attempts have been made to devise a system of movement notation. Some scholars believe that the ancient Egyptians made use of hieroglyphs to record dances and that the Romans employed a method of notation for salutatory gestures. However, the earliest known attempt, recorded in two manuscripts preserved in the Municipal Archives at Cervera, Spain, dates from the second half of the fifteenth century. Since that time, many other systems have appeared on the scene. Some were published and achieved a measure of use for a while but all, until the present day, fell eventually into disuse.

It is significant that music notation, which opened the way for the current highly developed state of the whole art of music, was first conceived in its modern form in the eleventh century but was not established as a uniform system till the mid-eighteenth. Dance notation got off to a much later start and has undergone a long succession of false tries.

That so many unsuccessful beginnings were made is not surprising. Movement is more complex than music because it exists in space as well as in time and because the body itself is capable of so many simultaneous modes of action. Consequently, the problems of formulating a movement notation that can be easily read and easily written are numerous.

Earlier methods had been outgrowths of phases in the development of dance itself and so all of them ultimately failed because the continual expansion of the dance vocabulary made each system, in turn, outmoded. The three fundamental problems - of recording complicated movement accurately, of recording it in economical and legible form, and of keeping up with continual innovations in movement - left dance notation in a state of flux, incapable of steady growth for centuries.

One of the first methods of notating dance - if it can be called a method - was the use of abbreviations for the names of steps; for example, r - reverencia; p - passo; de - double; re - represa. This method presupposed a knowledge of the steps, and hence its limitations are obvious.

The first book to make a visual attempt to describe dance is Thoinot Arbeau's "Orchesographie," published in 1588. The device Arbeau used was rather simple, as were the dances themselves. Written descriptions of positions and steps were accompanied by drawings and then given names. The notation consisted of these names being written opposite the corresponding musical note on which the step was made. Without Arbeau's lengthy explanations of the terms the dances are unintelligible.

The development of professional dancing during the time of Louis XIV produced a symbol form of notation. Raoul Feuillet first published his method, "Chorégraphie, ou l'Art de décrire la Danse," in 1700. This was followed by several "Recueil des Danses" containing compositions of Feuillet's as well as of Louis Pécourt's. Pécourt was a leading dancer and choreographer of the time. Thanks to Feuillet's notation we can study the steps on which the classical ballet grew but the system, though extremely well worked out, recorded little more than foot work and also lacked a clear indication of rhythm. It can be described as "track drawing," with the individual steps represented on a drawing of the floor pattern as made by the dancer. The book obviously met the needs of the period for it was translated into English and German and modifications of the system appeared throughout Europe until the end of the century. However, extensions of the Feuillet method, such as would be necessary to record, for example, movements of the torso, would have required great complexity in writing and difficulty in reading.

The next device appeared in 1852. Arthur Saint-Léon's system,

"Stenochorégraphie," combined stick figures with a musical staff for clarification. Another version of this system was brought out by Albert Zorn in 1887. Entitled "Grammar of the Art of Dancing," it attained a certain success and was used as a text book in dancing academies in Europe. In spite of apparent immediate advantages, stick figure notation has three distinct drawbacks: it is usually drawn from the audience's point of view, so that right and left have to be reversed by the dancer reading it; it cannot indicate the third dimension; and it gives position description rather than movement description. Indeed, to indicate timing, the writer must resort to the superimposition of music notes or counts, an awkward and uneconomical device.

The obvious need to indicate the accurate rhythm of movement led to the development of systems based on music notes. In the late nineteenth century, the most successful of these was that of Vladimir Stepanoff, dancer and teacher at the Imperial Maryinsky Theatre in St. Petersburg. The title of his book, "Alphabet des Mouvements du Corps Humain," published in 1891, indicates his attempt to record as much as possible of the movements of the whole body. However, the system was based mainly on the ballet vocabulary and this severely limited its usefulness.

The idea of adapting music notes to meet the needs of describing movement has remained popular, but it has become steadily clearer that notes are not sufficiently flexible to take care of the many needs in the field of movement. A highly individual development was Margaret Morris' book, "Notation of Movement," published in 1928. While there was a basis for her analysis of motion, the signs she chose were arbitrary, following no logical sequence and containing no provision for the indication of rhythm.

Until this time, the only staves used in the various systems were modifications of the music staff; horizontal lines, read from left to right. In 1928, Rudolf Laban published a new system of notation in which he introduced the vertical, symmetrical staff, read from the bottom up and clearly picturing, for the reader facing the score, right and left, front and back. The other invention which has made his system so flexible is using the length of the symbol on the staff to indicate duration of movement. These two innovations have made possible the first truly successful method of movement notation. Since Labanotation records in vividly legible form all possible movements of the body in space and time (and in a dimension heretofore unattempted - dynamics), it overcomes the obstacles which had impeded the progress of all earlier systems.

Because of his interest in movement in every phase of life - the street, the workshop, the theatre - it was inevitable that Laban should devise a system based not on any personal style but on the universal laws of kinetics. His early interests had led him to study all aspects of the theatrical arts. At twenty-five, he founded his own school in Munich where he developed his theories of forms of movement in space (choreutics) and of the qualities of movement (eukinetics). He later became director of movement at the Berlin State Opera and thereafter held similar posts at other state theatres. He then went to England where, with businessman F. C. Lawrence, he examined the movements of industrial workers, a study which resulted in his book "Effort. "

In the course of these varied activities, Laban formulated his notation system, Kinetographie Laban. Since the original text was published, tremendous strides have been made in the development of the system, and it has been applied to numerous non-dance fields of movement. Various dance centers and individuals both in America and abroad have added their contributions. Acting as a clearing house for ideas in the field of dance notation, the Dance Notation Bureau in New York has worked toward uniformity in Labanotation, sifting the most functional devices from those less useful and working to the elimination of local dialects. Today Labanotation is a system comparable to music notation in its universality, economy, and accuracy.

Introduction to Labanotation

Labanotation is a means of recording movement by means of symbols. Through this scientifically constructed method, all forms of movement, ranging from the simplest to the most complex, can be written. While its chief use to date has been in the field of dance, it is applicable to any field in which there is a need to record the motions of the human body.

Labanotation is, above all, a practical method. To understand its functions, we may compare them with the uses of music notation. In the areas of studying, teaching, composing, and performing, the musical score plays an important part. Because a great wealth of printed music is available, musicians have at their fingertips the work of many great composers. The conductor or performer, wherever he resides, can obtain a score from which he may play a long work of Beethoven or the newest ballet by Stravinsky. The student learns his instrument not only through the practice of exercises but also through playing the simpler classics presented in sheet music form. A parallel development in dance is just beginning. Through increased knowledge and use of Labanotation, its progress can be rapid.

The most obvious use of the system is that of recording choreography (or other movement) for preservation and future reconstruction. Because of the inadequacies of earlier methods, we cannot be certain, even upon a careful reading of Feuillet, for example, that we are performing the eighteenth-century court dances precisely as he intended. But we can be sure that generations to come will dance the works of contemporary choreographers exactly as they would wish. We know, because professional notators have watched the creation of these works; have marked the directions as they were given to the dancers at rehearsals; have changed the score whenever the choreographer changed his mind; have used a notation system capable of recording every particular of spatial design, timing, and dynamics; and have followed through until every role was on paper, completely and accurately. Each detail important to performance is written in full to insure correct reconstruction.

Yet, while Labanotation makes such minutely perfect reproduction possible, it can also be used when only a general outline of movement is required and leeway for personal interpretation is desirable. Notation does not confine the performer to stereotyped execution. It records what the choreographer feels to be essential and, since various composers differ in their demands, the notator may vary his treatment as indicated. Labanotation allows for any degree of specificity; this is one of its great practical assets.

How does this method of recording movement compare with the motion picture as a faithful recorder? Again, a comparison with music makes the point for notation. Recorded music has not obviated the printed sheet. Films have a unique advantage in the study of performance and for this they should be used unreservedly. But they reveal the choreography second-hand, through the dancer's interpretation; while, for the most part, it is the pure conception of the choreographer that Labanotation reconstructs. Notation alone is capable of recording his design exactly. Also, the advantage of easily accessible pencil and paper in contrast to expensive camera equipment and projection is undeniable.

Less obvious, but no less important as a function, is the use of Labanotation as a teaching aid. Its study should begin with the first lesson given in any movement form. Because the notation is based on a scientific analysis of the elements of movement, the student learns from it the nature of the component parts of the action he is to perform. When demonstrated, these are not always clearly visible; in writing they are completely unambiguous. Furthermore, any teacher, anywhere, can teach dance classics faithfully from a written score. Young dancers will thus be made aware of the richness of their art.

The establishment of a literature, authentic and unequivocal, may soon raise dance out of the realm of the minor arts. Labanotation is directed to the accomplishment of this end. Labanotation is not an isolated, abstract science. It is a practical science, a means to an end.

The aim of this book is to present the basic principles of Labanotation with a view to their practical application. The emphasis is on providing a firm foundation in the system, on which specialized skills may be built. The more detailed work in Labanotation has been introduced only briefly, so that some use of it may be made when the need arises. A second volume will deal more thoroughly with these more complex aspects. Later, specialized books will be prepared to meet the needs in different fields.

CHAPTER I

Fundamentals of Labanotation

THE BASIC APPROACH

If we understand the process of recording movement on paper - the conversion of the elements of space, time, and bodily motion into symbols which can be read back and reinterpreted into movement - we shall appreciate more fully the reasoning behind Labanotation and will understand why, in some instances, one analysis of movement was chosen in preference to another.

Because notation uses symbols, it has been likened to shorthand. This analogy is incorrect, since it is important that we notate in full everything that occurs in movement. The writer who is recording dance must always think in terms of the person who will read his score. If the notes are for personal use, then short cuts may be used. For dancers of the same background, it would be possible to omit certain obvious details of style, taking for granted that they would be understood and automatically performed. But a score prepared for general circulation must contain all the details necessary to accurate performance, so that it will be completely unambiguous regardless of the reader's personal knowledge or dance experiences.

The basic principle of Labanotation is that simple, natural movement is written in the most simple, direct way. The second premise is that everything that occurs is recorded. These two statements may seem contradictory. Actually, they are not, but we must know where to draw the line. Let us take an example. Walking is a simple, natural movement. Each person varies slightly in the manner in which he walks, but the basic process is the same.

The general pattern is uncomplicated, though the mechanical motions are really complex. The movements may be written in Labanotation in exact detail, as is sometimes necessary when a very stylized way of walking is desired.

But for general purposes we write only the essentials: The weight of the body moves forward by means of a step taken by one leg. This is the essence of the movement which anyone can understand. In most cases, no more need be indicated; we describe the basic form simply and directly, without fear of misunderstanding. Once we have a grasp of this essential pattern, we can quickly perceive those particular cases in which modifications or embellishments have been added, and we then know what extra detail must be written. By describing the pure form directly, we learn to understand the basic categories of movement and to distinguish the manipulations of them which are the sources of style.

PRINCIPLES OF MOVEMENT ANALYSIS

THE NATURE OF MOVEMENT

Movement is the result of the release of energy through muscular response to a stimulus (inner or outer). This response produces a visual result in space. In writing movement we do not record the stimulus. Nor do we record the muscular response. We record the visual result in space. Even when we are not moving, we are occupying space, and each part of the body can be given a spatial description.

MOVEMENT VERSUS POSITION

We describe movement by the path or way that it takes in space, using as milestones the absolute directions in space around us. As long as it does not stop, movement is continuous, and it is the movement between the points in space that we are describing. A position is a movement that has come to rest. Even to take a position, we must first move into it and then establish it by ceasing to move. Labanotation is a movement notation since the symbols represent movement, and absence of movement is shown by the absence of symbols.

ELEMENTS OF MOVEMENT

In order to record movement, we have to state exactly what occurs. This means reducing a movement to its basic elements. Any movement can be described in the following terms:

The PART OF THE BODY that moves (or several parts)

The use of SPACE (direction and level)

The TIMING of the movement (fast or slow)

The DYNAMICS, the texture of the movement (strong or light)

The pattern or FLOW in the movement (bound or free)

If all these elements are described as they are used, we have a complete picture of the desired movement. Sometimes, however, so full a description is not required. To some choreographers, spatial design and rhythm are all-important, the dancer being free to utilize dynamics to underline his own interpretation. In other cases, the essence of the choreography may lie in its special use of effort, and then the notation of dynamics is essential to a faithful recording of the plan. In industry, where much of the spatial pattern is dependent on the placement of the objects handled, use of flow is most significant. While the emphasis may differ, it is important to realize that all of these elements are applicable to any kind of movement, be it dance, sport, work, or everyday life.

THE STAFF

Labanotation uses a vertical, three-line staff. This staff represents the body. The center line of the staff is like a line drawn through the middle of the body, dividing right from left. The vertical columns at either side of the center line are used for the various parts of the body.

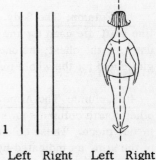

Left Right   Left Right

Only the three basic lines are used in Labanotation. For the sake of clarity at this stage, however, the following description of the use of the columns uses dotted lines to define the areas within and beyond the three basic lines.

USE OF THE COLUMNS

1st Column: Supports. Immediately next to the center line are the support columns. Here are written the symbols indicating movements of parts of the body that take over weight, i. e. , act as supports. We assume the normal way of supporting the body to be on the feet, and so a direction symbol in a support column means a step taken in that direction. The weight can also be taken over by the knees, hips, hands - even the head. In these cases, the specific signs for these parts appear in one or the other support column.

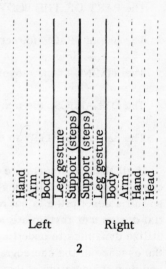

2nd Column: Leg Gestures. Adjacent to the support columns are the columns for leg gestures. By gesture we mean a movement in space that does not carry weight. A direction symbol in these columns describes a movement of the whole leg, moving in one piece. The individual parts of the leg - the thigh, lower leg, and foot - are also written in these columns as indicated by the specific signs for those parts.

3rd Column: The Body. The columns just outside of the three-line staff are used for the body. The column on the right side is used for the chest; the one on the left side is used for the pelvic girdle and for the whole torso.

4th Column: The Arms. A direction symbol placed in one or the other fourth column shows a movement for the whole arm, moving in one piece. These columns are also used for the individual parts of the arm, as indicated by the specific signs for those parts.

5th Column: The Hands. The next columns out from the arm columns are used for the hands. Since the movements of the hands can be described in so many different ways, the specific signs for the hands are always used to indicate the difference between a movement of the hand in general and the use of the palm, fingers, and other parts.

6th Column: The Head. Additional Columns. The head is written on the right side, adjacent to the hand column. Supplementary columns, extending out, can be used where need be, much as ledger lines are used in music. These are employed for additional symbols modifying the main movement indicated.

THE DIRECTION SYMBOLS

The basic symbol is a rectangle. This indicates no direction; that is, directly above, at, or below your center of weight. We call this position "in place."

By changing the shape of this basic symbol, we indicate direction.

Forward

To the right

THE EIGHT MAIN DIRECTIONS

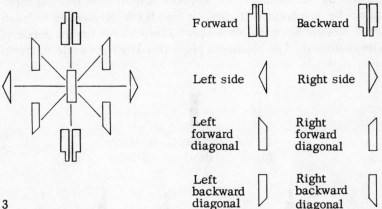

Forward	Backward
Left side	Right side
Left forward diagonal	Right forward diagonal
Left backward diagonal	Right backward diagonal

3

Note that there are two symbols for the directions forward and back, one for the right side of the staff and one for the left.

As you rest this book on the table in front of you, the forward symbol points to your forward direction, the right symbol points to your right, and so on. The diagonal directions are exactly between forward and side or side and backward. We use the word diagonal for these directions in space and not for a slanting upward or downward movement which we describe in terms of level.

These are the main directions around the body. Movement often employs variations of these, in-between-directions, as they are called. These minor distinctions may be left until later.

Labanotation views direction from the body. The body is so constructed that we have a right side and a left, a front and a back. This is constant, and so we describe direction as being forward from the body or backward from the body; to the right or to the left of it. This means that if we turn to face another direction in space, say another part of the room or stage, we still judge forward, backward, or side from our own body. Body direction is given predominance over stage direction. This holds true in Labanotation with very few exceptions which we will discuss when they arise.

INDICATION OF LEVEL

The level of movement - upward, downward, or horizontal - is indicated by the shading of the symbol. A movement into any direction can be on a horizontal, low, or high level. Straight up is "place high." Straight down is "place low." Down moves toward gravity; up away from it. The horizontal plane lies at a right angle to these.

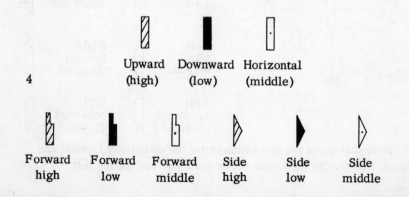

Upward (high)   Downward (low)   Horizontal (middle)

4

Forward high   Forward low   Forward middle   Side high   Side low   Side middle

PLACING THE DIRECTION SYMBOLS ON THE STAFF

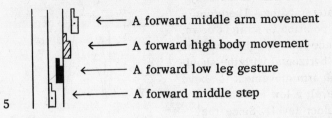

← —— A forward middle arm movement

← —— A forward high body movement

← —— A forward low leg gesture

←——— A forward middle step

5

The placement of the movement symbols on the body staff shows which part of the body does that movement.

ANALYSIS OF DIRECTION AND LEVEL

Middle Support. When we stand with our feet together, we are supporting ourselves "in place"; that is, our supports are directly underneath our center of weight. The normal standing position places the weight on the whole foot, with the legs straight, but not taut or stiff-kneed. This normal standing position is written as "place middle."

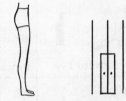

6a   Place middle

Low Support. A low support occurs when the body is lowered through bending (flexing) the knees. In a low support the weight is also on the whole foot. This is written as "place low."

6b   Place low

High Support. A high support occurs when the body is raised by lifting through the foot. The weight is supported on the ball of the foot. This is "place high."

6c   Place high

Gestures. The arm normally
hangs down by the side of the body
when you are standing. Therefore,
its normal position is straight down;
that is, place low. Middle level for
the arm is horizontal with the shoulder. A high arm movement is above
shoulder level; a low movement is
below shoulder level. Since the
whole arm moves from the shoulder joint, its relation to the shoulder determines both its direction and its level in space.

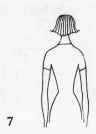

7

Levels for the Arms. Examples shown are for the right arm.

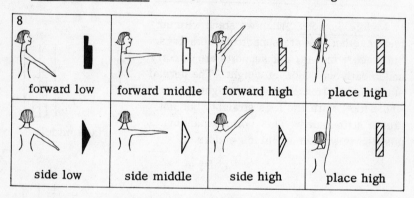

Levels for the Legs. The whole leg moves from the hip joint,
and so its relation to the hip determines the direction and level of
the movement. Examples shown are for the right leg.

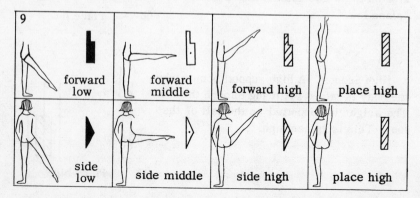

TIMING

The staff lines, read from the bottom up, indicate the flow of time. This time line is marked off into regular beats. Indications written one after the other are performed sequentially in time. Indications written side by side occur simultaneously.

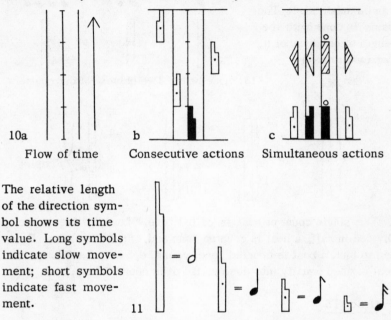

10a Flow of time   b Consecutive actions   c Simultaneous actions

The relative length of the direction symbol shows its time value. Long symbols indicate slow movement; short symbols indicate fast movement.

11

The basic length chosen for a beat in writing a movement sequence will depend on the needs. Detailed movements usually require a longer basic unit.

STATEMENT OF BASIC LENGTH

At the beginning of a piece, the basic length should be indicated.

12

For general purposes, one beat, the quarter note in music (♩), is represented by four squares on graph paper. We use graph paper as an aid to consistency in indicating rhythms. For the beginner, graph paper of six squares to the inch is most practical. Later eight squares to the inch, or even ten, may be used.

BREAKDOWN OF A COUNT (BEAT)

One count in music can be subdivided. The same is done with the length of one symbol in Labanotation.

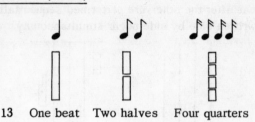

13   One beat   Two halves   Four quarters

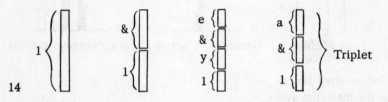

14

The single count or beat is called "one," "two," "three," etc. Divided in half, a beat is counted "one and," "two and," etc. Divided in four, a beat is counted "one, y, and, e," etc. A triplet is one beat divided equally into three parts. It is counted "one, and, a."

UPBEATS

An upbeat belongs to the previous measure and is used as a preparation for the next measure. Many pieces of music start with an upbeat. In movement, we often use a small preparatory motion before the main one starts: bending the legs before a jump; drawing the arm back before a throw. When we count "and one" it is as though we had silently counted out the previous measure: "(one, two, three, four) and one."

METRONOME INDICATION

Where exact tempi are required, metronome indications should be stated. This is the same indication that appears in music - the number of beats per minute: ♩ = 60. ♩ = 112. In a dance score this indication is placed at the beginning to the left of the staff.

bered on the left, outside the count marks. In dance scores, these numbers tie in with the numbered music bars of the rehearsal score. In the last example, which shows two bars of 6/8 time, the music counts have been written in the first bar. On the outside, the dancer's counts have been indicated in parentheses. Usually a 6/8 is too fast for the dancer to count each beat, and so only the main accents, two in each bar, are numbered. You should be aware of when you are counting metrically and when not.

CLARIFICATIONS

Since an understanding of the idea of "place" is so fundamental to the study of Labanotation, a little more detailed exposition is in order.

<u>WHERE IS PLACE?</u>

Have you
been introduced
to PLACE?

Do you know
WHERE
PLACE
is?

PLACE
is
NOT
WHERE YOU WERE

MARKING OFF THE BARS OF MUSIC

The vertical dance staff (like the horizontal music staff) is marked off into bars (measures). Since the relative length of the symbols is so important, it is necessary that all the bars be the same length. Here are examples of bars marked off into different rhythms, (read the dance staff, as always, from the bottom up):

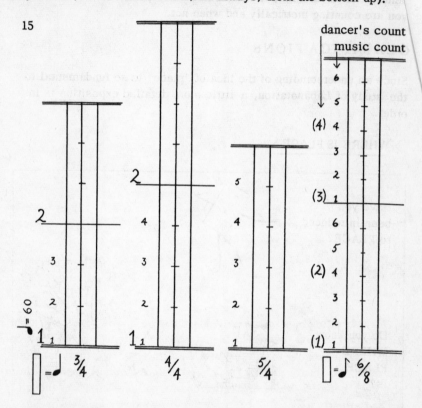

Note the use of lines. The counts (beats) are marked off on the center line with short strokes. The bars are marked off with lines extending beyond the three-line staff. A section is marked at the beginning and at the end with double lines.

Note the use of numerals. The counts are numbered on the left side. These are often not indicated unless the movement is tricky and they are needed as a guide to rhythm. The bars are also num-

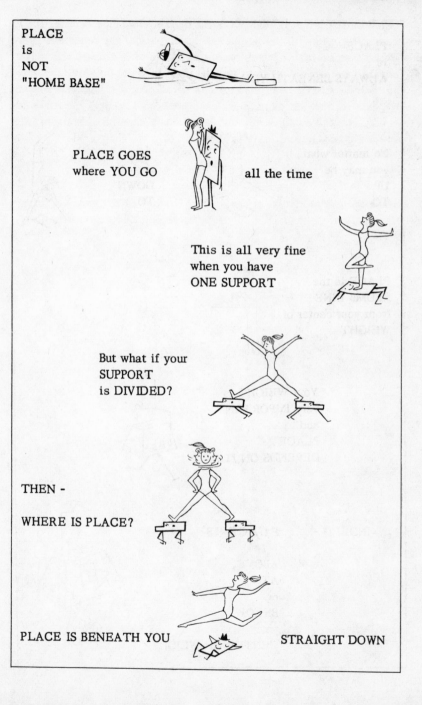

PLACE
is
NOT
"HOME BASE"

PLACE GOES
where YOU GO   all the time

This is all very fine
when you have
ONE SUPPORT

But what if your
SUPPORT
is DIVIDED?

THEN -

WHERE IS PLACE?

PLACE IS BENEATH YOU   STRAIGHT DOWN

PLACE
is
ALWAYS BENEATH YOU

No matter what
you may be
UP
TO

or
DOWN
TO

PLACE is the
PLUMB LINE
from your center of
WEIGHT

Your WEIGHT is
very IMPORTANT
and
PLACE
DEPENDS ON IT

LBS

INDEED -   PLACE IS:

ABOVE,
AT,
or
BELOW
your
CENTER OF WEIGHT

LBS

CHAPTER II

Steps and Arm Movements

SUPPORTS AND STEPS WITH USE OF LEVELS

IN "PLACE"

Note on reading: When the weight is on one foot, the other is free, just clear of the ground, as in ordinary walking.

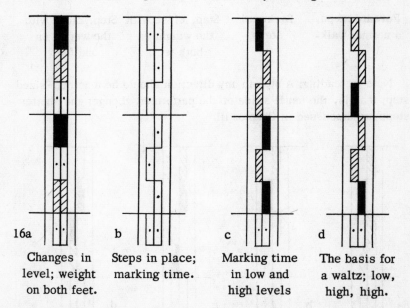

16a	b	c	d
Changes in level; weight on both feet.	Steps in place; marking time.	Marking time in low and high levels	The basis for a waltz; low, high, high.

In performing Figs. (b), (c) and (d), the weight should be transferred completely from one foot to the other, the free foot being just clear of the ground.

FORWARD AND BACKWARD STEPS

Direction symbols in the support columns indicate that the body is moved away from its original stance into the given direction by means of a step on the right or left leg. Each step means a progression of the whole body in which the weight is transferred until it is vertically above the new point of support.

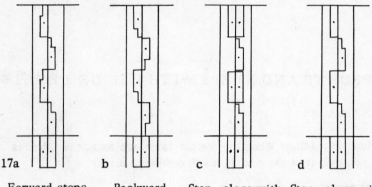

17a	b	c	d
Forward steps, a normal walk.	Backward steps	Step, close with the weight on both feet.	Step, close with the weight on one foot.

Note on reading: A step in any direction should be a normal-sized step; that is, the usual stride of the performer. Longer and shorter steps are discussed in Chapter III.

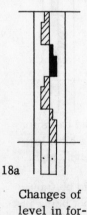 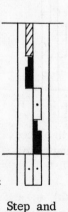 

18a	b	c	d
Changes of level in forward steps	Swaying forward and back	Step and change of level	Swaying backward and forward with change in level

STEPS TO THE SIDE

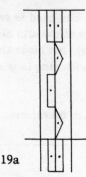

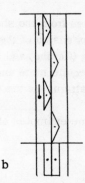

19a

Step side, close, step side,
close with feet together.

b

Continuous steps to the side,
crossing in front and then in back.

In Fig. 19 (b) the black pin is used to show the relationship of the two legs as the step across is taken. The point of the pin is the indicator, not the head:

in front: ↓   in back: ↑

DIAGONAL STEPS

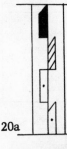

20a	b	c	d
Forward right diagonal	Forward left diagonal	Backward right diagonal	Backward left diagonal

All the walking steps should be done facing the same direction in the room. Turning the body to face a new direction will be discussed later. Steps to the side should be made to the side of the body, not facing the side of the room. Diagonal steps should also be taken with the body facing front. Do not give in to the temptation to make a slight turn and walk forward into the diagonal of the room.

MOVEMENTS OF THE WHOLE ARM

The arm moves from the shoulder in one piece. The hand is carried along as an extension of the arm. Most gestures of the arm also include bending (flexing) and stretching (extending), but since these movements require more analysis we will deal with simple gestures and spatial patterns for the time being.

Below are some examples of everyday uses of arm movements.

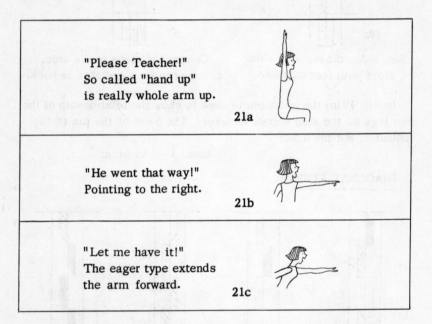

"Please Teacher!"
So called "hand up"
is really whole arm up.

21a

"He went that way!"
Pointing to the right.

21b

"Let me have it!"
The eager type extends
the arm forward.

21c

CARRIAGE OF THE ARMS

The arm is normally relaxed with a soft, not stiff elbow. If you let your arm fall down by your side as you stand, you will see that it is neither bent nor stretched. To move it forward, merely raise it in space as it is; do not make any extra motion of stretching or bending it. These would be additions to the basic movement, and we want first of all to become acquainted with the simplest, most natural way of moving the arm in space. (See additional notes later in this chapter.)

PATH IN SPACE

As the arm moves from one direction to another, it describes a path in space. Unless a deviation is shown, the arm should go directly from one position to the other. This may mean an automatic flexing of the arm. This flexing should not be exaggerated, for it occurs only to facilitate the movement of the arm along the designated path. This is more easily felt when the movement has to be done quickly. You will find that, to reach your destination rapidly, you will do the right thing naturally.

<u>Direct Path.</u>

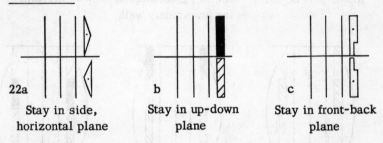

22a	b	c
Stay in side, horizontal plane	Stay in up-down plane	Stay in front-back plane

<u>Indirect Path.</u> Very often the above destinations are deliberately reached via another direction:

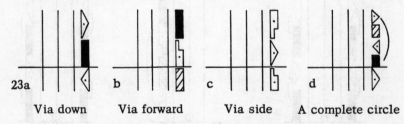

23a	b	c	d
Via down	Via forward	Via side	A complete circle

To perform a circular arm movement in space, it is necessary to write at least four direction symbols so that no corners will be cut. The phrasing of the movement can be shown by using a bow, as in music. See Fig. 23 (d).

Note on reading: When there is no movement written for the arm, it stays where it is, in the direction to which it last moved. The absence of symbols means absence of movement.

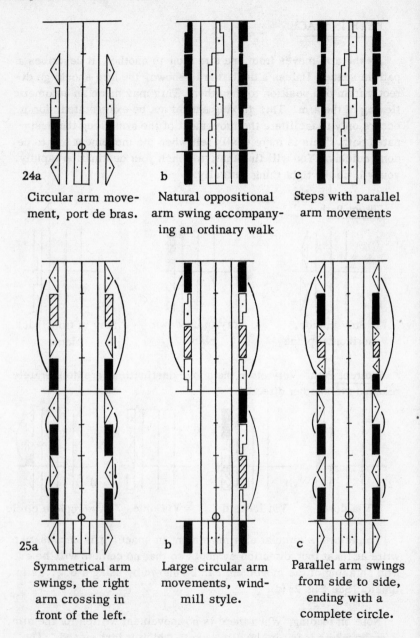

24a Circular arm movement, port de bras.

b Natural oppositional arm swing accompanying an ordinary walk

c Steps with parallel arm movements

25a Symmetrical arm swings, the right arm crossing in front of the left.

b Large circular arm movements, windmill style.

c Parallel arm swings from side to side, ending with a complete circle.

The symbol O in the support column means that you stand where you are. Further explanations are given in Chapter IV.

STUDY IN STEPS WITH ARM MOVEMENTS

Suggested music: "Jeanie with the Light Brown Hair."

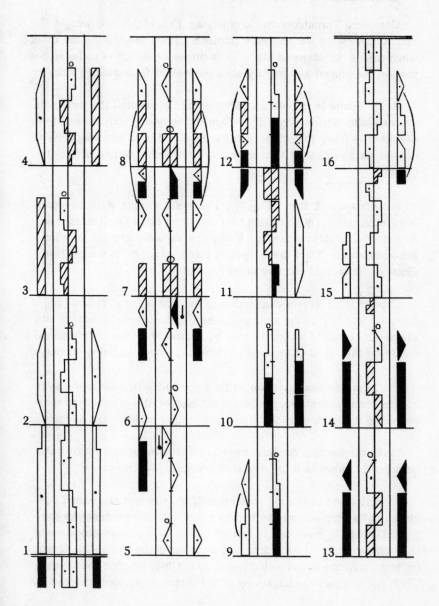

CLARIFICATIONS

TAKING STEPS

<u>Complete Transference</u>. In studying Fig. 16 (b), the weight should have been transferred completely from one foot to the other when taking the steps in place. A common tendency is to leave both feet on the ground and merely shift the weight from side to side.

<u>Rule:</u> Symbols in both support columns mean that the weight is on both feet, divided equally. When the weight is only on one foot, the other is free, just clear of the ground. This is what happens in normal walking; as we take each step, the leg is released from the ground.

<u>Breakdown of a Step</u>. Fig. 17 (a) shows a simple walk in a forward direction. This action of taking steps is so familiar that we do not usually think about it. Every day we walk forward in order to get somewhere. Only under special circumstances do we become aware of the actual process of taking a step.

Labanotation uses a convention in the writing of simple steps; a direction symbol in the support column indicates the direction into which our center of weight travels by means of a step. We also indicate by this symbol the level in which the body is being supported.

For future reference, it would be a good idea to look at the symbol that represents a step to see what part of the process is represented in the beginning of the symbol, in the middle, and at the end.

In the diagram on the next page, two simple forward steps have been broken down into the different sections of movement.

To define the beginning and the end, we say that the actual beginning of a step occurs at the moment when the foot contacts the ground. This is most easily felt when you have to take quick steps right on the beat. If each step had to be accented, as in tap dance, for instance, the sound would come as the foot touches the floor. Thus, we see that the beginning of the direction symbol, marked (b),

is the moment of contact with the floor.
Before this can happen, however, we must
make a small preparatory movement, extending the leg forward in space and also
carrying the weight on the standing leg into
the forward direction so that the transfer
will be smooth. This preparation for a step
is assumed and takes place before the
count - see (a) in the diagram. The section
marked (c) is the point at which the weight
is being transferred from one foot to the
other, and so for a moment the weight is
supported equally on both feet. In (d) the
weight has been completely transferred over
to the front foot. The other leg is then ready
to make the preparation (a) for the next step.

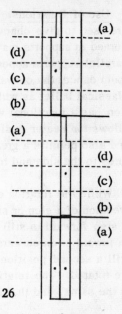

(a) - preparation for step
(b) - contact with the ground
(c) - transference in progress
(d) - transference completed

TURNED OUT OR NOT?

One of the first questions to come up is whether the standing
position and the steps are to be performed with the feet parallel or
with a "turn out"; that is, with the outward rotation of the leg.

Simple steps should be performed in a simple, natural way. It is
not natural to be turned out, nor is it natural to be turned in. Therefore, until the exact amount of leg rotation or the specific placement
of the feet is indicated, the steps and positions should be performed
in the way that is natural. This differs according to the individual's
build and his previous training. For this reason, Labanotation does
not label one thing as being "the natural position." When we want
to designate an exact degree of rotation, we can use special signs
to do so. But until you see such directions, use the position that
feels normal and comfortable for you.

Use of Rotations. In supports and steps, rotations of the legs are used to give character, style, or expression to the movement. Turned in supports may give a grotesque or comic effect; the use of parallel supports appears in many primitive dances and also in ballroom dance; the outward rotation of the legs is a necessary part of classical ballet as well as other forms of dance. The outward rotation has a functional value which must not be overlooked since it allows for neater positions of the feet (fifth position in particular) and also permits a greater range of movement; for example, leg gestures to the side and to the back.

While the rotation of the legs will change the character and expression of a step or support, it does not change the basic structure. A step forward is still a step forward, whether it is performed with an inward or an outward rotation. A second position (feet apart) is still a second position regardless of the manner in which the legs are rotated. The relation of your supports to your center of weight is the same, and that is the fundamental thing.

Rotation the Basic Movement. It is a different matter when the rotation of the limb is the basic movement. This often occurs when the position or direction of the limb in space is already established and the rotation is made as a distinct action. In such cases, other movements, such as flexing and extending, become the additional features. Once more we must stress the need to distinguish movement in terms of what is basic and functional as against what is added, or ornamentation.

NOTES ON PERFORMANCE

Steps: Pictorial Indication of the Symbol. A common error made by beginners is to think that the direction symbols pictorially represent the feet. They feel that the oblong shape of the place symbol looks like the foot, or that the direction indicator represents the direction into which the big toe should point.

[symbol] = [feet top view]   [symbol] = [foot]   [symbol] = [foot]   [symbol] = [foot side view]

27   this . . . . is . . . . . . all . . . . wrong.

Because of this misconception, the beginner tends to read everything with parallel feet until he comes to the steps to the side where he gets confused. (We don't know how he would interpret backward steps, following this logic!)

Remember: The shape of the direction symbol indicates pure direction. Only when we place the direction symbols on the staff do we describe the part of the body that uses that direction. In the case of supports, the direction symbols do not describe the rotation of the leg, which makes the foot point in a specific direction. Rather they tell the direction into which the center of weight travels when a step is taken. They describe the movement of the support away from a previous position.

<u>Arm Movements: Facing of the Palms.</u> In a gesture with the arm, the use of the palm and the direction in which it faces can change the whole expression of the movement. It is important to understand the normal way to carry the hand; that is, the normal way for the palm to face.

When your arms hang down by your side, the palms face in, toward the body. You could say that the palms face one another, overlooking the fact that the body is in between. If you raise your arms forward to middle level (horizontal), the palms will still face in toward one another. As you lift the arms up to place high, overhead, the palms still face in toward one another. There has been no change in this respect from the starting position.

28a    b 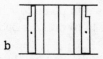   c

Palms face in   Palms face in   Palms face in

But these examples raise the question of where the palms face.

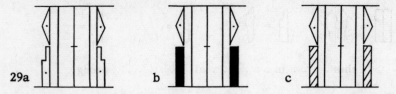

29a   b   c

The problem arises because people do not all agree on where the palms should face when the arms are held out to the side. Some say they should face down; some say up; some say forward; and even others say that it all depends on where the arms came from. Out of all this, we must find a simple, universally acceptable position.

In Labanotation we say that the palms face forward when the arms are held out to the side. Let us see why. In Fig. 30 the arms move up via side middle and then down again the same way.

Starting position: The arms are down with the palms facing in.

(1) As the arms are lifted naturally to the side, there is a slight but constant rotation outward, so that when the arm is horizontal the palms are facing forward.

(2) This slight, imperceptible rotation continues as the arms are raised to place high with the result that the palms end facing in toward each other, just as we found in Fig. 28 (c).

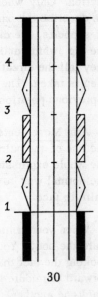

30

(3) The arms are lowered to side middle, a slight inward rotation occurs, bringing the palms to face forward again.

(4) As the arms are dropped to place low, the slight inward rotation brings the palms facing in toward the body again.

Your reaction to this analysis may be: Is it natural to include an arm rotation, no matter how small? Is not this rotation already an added feature? If so, let us reconsider the movements in Fig. 30 and try to perform them without any rotation whatever.

Starting position: The same; palms facing in.

(1) Palms would face down.

(2) Palms would face out, away from each other. Does this look or feel natural?

Try it! The arms have a definite twisted feeling. In fact, the moment you relax the muscles, the hands automatically rotate to their normal state - palms in.

It is of interest to note that when we bring the arms up overhead from side middle, the slight rotations used produce the same result as bringing them up from forward middle where there was no need for any rotation at all.

CHAPTER III

Variations in Steps and Arm Gestures, Positions of the Feet

USE OF RHYTHMS

STEPS IN DIFFERENT RHYTHMS

The use of different timing (meter) is indicated in the figures below. The last, 5/4, is not so common but has been introduced for practice.

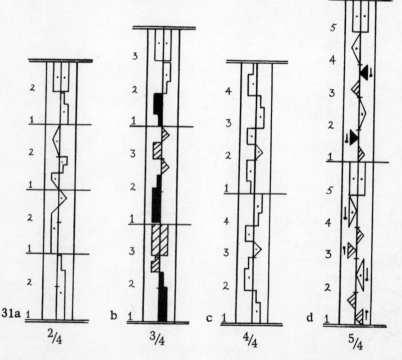

CONTRASTS IN THE USE OF RHYTHMS

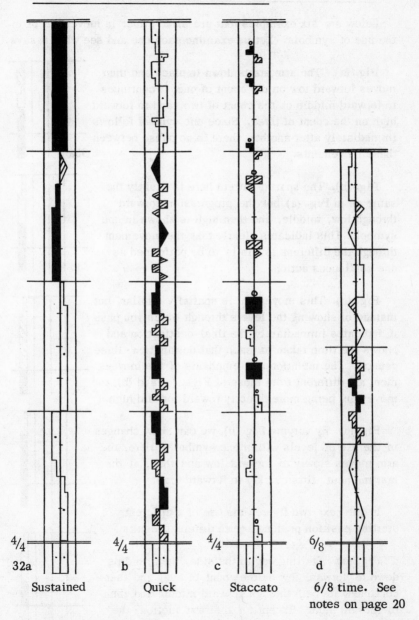

$^4/_4$	$^4/_4$	$^4/_4$	$^6/_8$
32a	b	c	d
Sustained	Quick	Staccato	6/8 time. See
			notes on page 20

Repeat each one until a smooth performance is achieved.

RHYTHMS IN ARM MOVEMENTS

Below are six examples that are alike either in movement or in the use of symbols. Let us examine each one and see what it says.

Fig. (a). The arm starts down in place and then moves forward low on the count of one; it continues to forward middle on the count of two, and to forward high on the count of three. Since one symbol follows immediately after another, there is no pause between these movements.

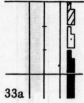

33a

Fig. (b). The spatial pattern here is exactly the same as in Fig. (a) but the progression forward through low, middle, and then high is shown in one symbol. This indicates clearly that the movement through the different levels is to be performed as one continuous action.

33b

Fig. (c). This movement is spatially similar, but instead of showing the levels through which you pass it indicates immediately the final destination and shows the time taken to reach that destination - three counts. The intention and emphasis of the movement are different from those of Figs. (a) and (b), the movement being more directly toward forward high.

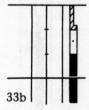

33c

Fig. (d). By varying Fig. (b), we can show changes in the use of levels within one symbol. Here, the arm moves slowly to forward low and then, at the last moment, lifts quickly to forward high.

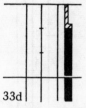

33d

In the next two figures the use of a different starting position produces quite different results.

Fig. (e). Starting out to the side, the arm dips down to forward low on the count of one, and then continues its path through forward middle and then to forward high. Except for the first motion, the movement is the same as that in Fig. (b).

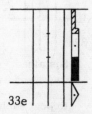

33e

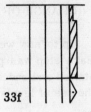

Fig. 33 (f). Here the arm starts at the side and moves on a direct path to its destination, forward high in three counts. The directions forward-low and forward-middle are not used; therefore, except for the final position reached, this movement has no relation to Fig. 33 (c).

33f

Legato and Staccato. Below are examples of a spatial pattern performed in an increasingly staccato manner.

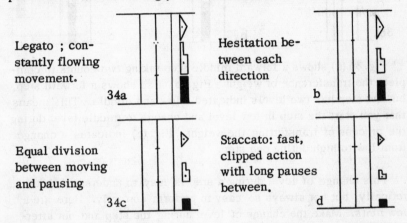

Legato ; con-
stantly flowing
movement.

34a

Hesitation be-
tween each
direction

b

Equal division
between moving
and pausing

34c

Staccato: fast,
clipped action
with long pauses
between.

d

Change of Level Within a Symbol. Note the difference in drawing between one symbol with a change in level and two symbols following one another closely. In the case of two symbols there is a separation between them large enough to be clearly visible but not so large as to make a rhythmical change. In drawing one symbol there is no break at all, and the relative length of the indicator is greater.

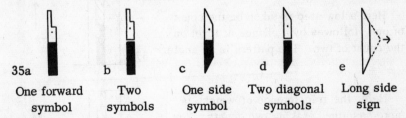

35a

One forward
symbol

b

Two
symbols

c

One side
symbol

d

Two diagonal
symbols

e

Long side
sign

Note the drawing of the side symbol in Fig. (c). Elongated side symbols are not drawn to a point, the center is flattened out, leaving the side indicators at top and bottom, as indicated in Fig. (e).

CHANGE OF LEVEL DURING A STEP

Up to now we have taken steps in high, middle, and low level. Each step was performed on one level; that is, the transference started and ended in the same level. It is possible, however to vary the use of levels during the process of taking a step.

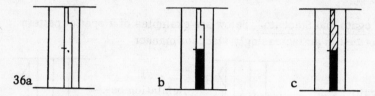

Fig. 36 (a) shows a forward middle step taking two counts to complete the transference of weight. Fig. (b) also shows a forward step, but the step has two levels indicated - low and middle. This means that you start the step in low level and change to middle level during the process of transferring the weight. Fig. (c) indicates a change from low to high during one step.

This change of level during a step is easy to understand theoretically, but not always so easy to perform correctly. Here are a few hints. Make the change of level during the step and not afterwards, as though you had changed your mind half way through. Think of very fluent steps such as you would use in a lilting waltz where the transitions are very smooth. There should be no angular movement at all. Note the difference in the path of the movement in the two examples below.

Here a low step is taken on the count of one, followed by a change of level on the count of two. The pattern is an angle.

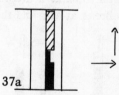

Here, the transference of weight is more sustained, taking two counts. You are still moving forward as you are rising so that the space pattern is a curve.

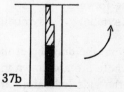

LENGTH OF STEPS

The length of an ordinary step in any direction, as we have said, should be the average pace or stride of the performer. The exact amount of space covered will vary according to the individual build. When a step shorter or longer than the average is required, an appropriate pre-sign is placed before the direction symbol. These pre-signs are like adjectives; they modify the nature of the subject; in this case, the step - short forward step; long side step.

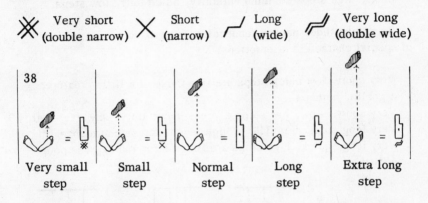

The direction symbol is shortened by the amount of space taken by the pre-sign (usually one square of graph paper), but the pre-sign should be read as part of the direction symbol for purposes of time value of the movement. In the examples below, each group of symbols has the same time value.

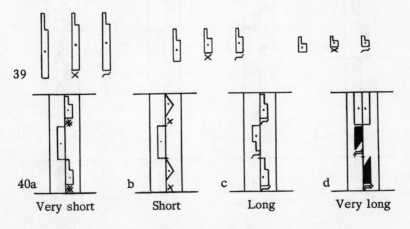

INDICATIONS OF STYLE IN STEPS

By combining changes in the length of steps with the use of different rhythms, we can add character and style to simple steps. This is the first instance so far in our study of Labanotation in which we can recognize some of the qualities inherent in movement. Here are some of the results of different combinations of time and space.

Short steps tend to be quick. Long steps tend to be slow.
Short, high steps combine naturally, as do long, low steps.

By mixing these natural tendencies, we produce steps indicative of special characters or emotions:

Very short, low quick steps are like those of a little creature, a goblin, perhaps.
Very short, slow, low steps express uncertainty, shyness, fear.
Very long steps in middle or high level express confidence.
Very long, quick, high steps are like a strut and express pomposity.

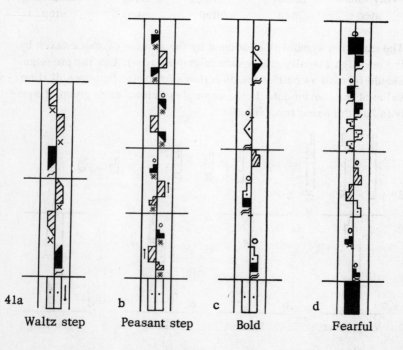

41a Waltz step   b Peasant step   c Bold   d Fearful

CLOSED POSITIONS OF THE FEET

FIRST POSITION

The normal standing position with the heels together is called first position. To serve our immediate purpose, which is to show the different relations of the legs when supporting in place, the feet in the diagrams to the right are shown to be turned out.

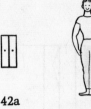

42a

THIRD POSITION

This position is basically the same as first in that the supports are directly beneath the center of weight - in place. The difference lies in the relation of the two supports; one is diagonally in front of the other. (Remember; the point of the pin does the indicating; not the head.) The position can be described from the point of view of the front leg or the back, depending on which is the active or important one.

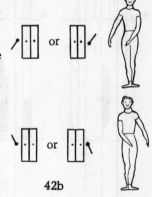

42b

FIFTH POSITION

This is again basically the same as first position, the supports both being in place, but here one of the supports is directly in front of the other. A fifth position can also be described as having the right leg in front or the left leg in back. The fifth position is associated especially with classical ballet where it is performed with an extreme turn-out. The open positions of the feet - second and fourth - are discussed in the next chapter.

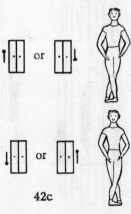

42c

STUDY IN LENGTH OF STEPS AND RHYTHMS

Suggested music: "Skaters' Waltz."

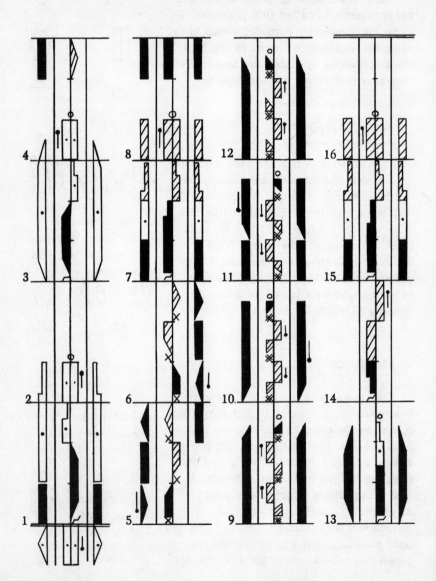

CLARIFICATIONS

The study of rhythm in movement is one that never really ends because there are endless variations in its use by different parts of the body and in different types of movement. For our purposes at this stage, it is important to start with a thorough and accurate understanding of the fundamentals of rhythm, so we suggest that, after reading through this chapter, you review the explanations given in Chapter I.

NOTES ON READING

Read through the various examples in this chapter again, working on each one, phrase by phrase, until the right use of rhythms and the arresting or flow of movement comes out naturally. To get the most out of each example, it is best to commit it to memory. Since it is not easy to read at the same time that you are moving and dancing, the need to focus your eyes on a book may result in stilted movement. Once you know the patterns, check the notation for details of performance, particularly the use of timing. It is important that you develop good reading habits at an early stage, and so we suggest the following as a practical way to tackle a new piece:

1. Glance over the whole piece to get a quick idea of the use of rhythm, of the body, of direction and level. As you progress, you will learn to recognize quickly the type of movement involved.

2. Read through the piece slowly to explore the use of space and time. You should now have a good idea of the style indicated.

3. Start to translate the symbols into movement, working on one phrase at a time. A phrase may be one measure, perhaps two. In some cases, the phrasing of the movements may not coincide with the bar lines at all.

4. As you work on each phrase, repeat it until it ceases to be a group of isolated motions and becomes, rather, related movement pattern. When you have mastered one phrase, go on to the next. Then perform one phrase after the other until the sequence is well established.

Two points in particular will help you to speed up the process of
learning to perform written movement. One is to anticipate what is
coming next; the other is to sense which are the main movements
and which are merely transitions or preparations.

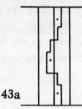

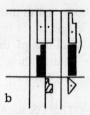

43a

b

Anticipate the change in direction in the third
step by preparing the weight to move backward after it has been traveling forward.

An upbeat prepara-
tion for the subse-
quent movement

CHANGES IN TIMING: THEIR EFFECT ON MOVEMENT

Timing is an integral part of movement - you cannot divorce it
from the other elements. Two movements may use the same spatial patterns and the same parts of the body, but if one is fast and
the other slow they are not identical; different qualities will appear.

When a movement is slow and there is plenty of time at your dis-
posal, you indulge in the use of space and weight as you cannot do
when there is little time and you must hurry. Consider simple
jumps. In a comfortably timed jump you take ample time for the
preparation, sufficient time in the air, and enough time on the landing to prepare for the next jump. If the tempo is too slow, you become heavy, earth-bound, and can hardly rise into the air at all.
If the tempo is speeded up, you will have less time for your preparation and less time in the air. If the tempo is extremely fast, there
will be no time for leg action at all; you will scarcely rise from
the ground. Indeed, at best, you will succeed in achieving only a
nervous, bounce-like motion. The expenditure of energy is changed
according to the tempo of the movement. Less energy is needed to
perform a jump in the time range to which it is best suited.

Observe what happens to a swinging movement when the tempo
becomes too slow or too fast. A natural swing, which uses gravity
and the weight of the body correctly, contains much free flowing

movement. If the same spatial pattern is slowed down, it must resist the force of gravity in order to be slow and hence must be carefully guided. If the same spatial pattern is speeded up, the same holds true, for, in order to cover space very quickly, the natural use of gravity and of the weight of the body must be not only ignored but fought against. The quality of the movement is changed: the element of energy must be added and any softness or relaxed, free-flowing movement disappears completely.

Thus we see that a change in timing can mean a whole change in the quality and texture of movement. For example, a gliding movement becomes a darting action when it is quickened; a punch becomes a slow, pressing movement when it is retarded. Consideration of the quality and content of movement in terms of the use of energy, weight, and flow is a study in itself. At this point it is important only that you be aware of the existence of these elements in order to observe them and to recreate them when necessary.

To know the exact speed of a piece of music, the metronome figure must be indicated. The same is true of Labanotation. For exactness, the metronome marking should be included in a score. But for general practice it is better for the individual to sense the appropriate timing for a piece. Leeway should be left for a certain amount of individual interpretation. As you read each new piece, remember that your first impression of the movement may not have been correct. You may have read it too slowly while you were just beginning to familiarize yourself with the spatial pattern. At the right tempo the movements may take on a different expression and meaning.

DETERMINING LENGTH OF STEP

The length of a step must be a relative thing. We cannot state that a normal-sized step will be 12 inches, and short or long steps so many inches accordingly. There can be no tape-measure rule. The key to the size of steps should not lie in the distance  between the foot prints, but rather in the movement used to take the step - the action of the legs and the traveling of the center of weight.

Another clue to the size of a step lies in the use of energy, the effort or lack of effort used in taking a step. Long steps are often the result of the enjoyment to be had in expending energy. Short steps may be the result of a reluctance to use energy. In short, our analysis of the length of steps should rest partly on the desired expression.

CORRECT USE OF THE RELATIONSHIP PINS

Do not confuse the relationship pin "in front": with the direction "forward": .

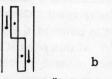

44a

b

c

The pins mean "in front"; the steps are in place.

Forward steps are written with forward symbols.

Forward steps in front of the body; exact center forward, as in tightrope walking.

Remember to write the pin for the active leg, since this makes for more logical reading. In Fig. 45, the left leg moves into place, therefore the pin should be written next to the symbol for the left leg.

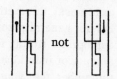

not

45

HOW TO PERFORM CERTAIN MOVEMENTS

Sustained Movement. One of the difficult things to perform properly, especially without a teacher on hand to observe and correct, is sustained movement, in particular a sustained step. When an elementary student first reads a piece, the initial version is often a jerky, wooden rendition of the desired movement patterns. This is understandable. The student sees a forward symbol and rushes into that direction. It is only on the second and third reading that he becomes aware of the time value and makes the necessary adjustments in performance. Arm movements in particular are apt to be done in a rigid manner. Sometimes the arms are raised stiffly, like those of wooden soldiers. Try to retain the natural, relaxed position of the arm as it is when it hangs down in place.

Below are two examples of movements that are frequently performed incorrectly. In each case, the second figure shows a mistaken performance of the first.

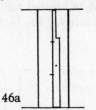

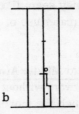

A sustained step. Take three counts to transfer the weight completely.

Instead, the student takes a step on the first count and holds the last two. (o is a hold weight sign, described in the next chapter.)

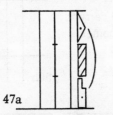

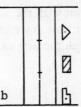

A fluent arm circle showing continuous movement.

Instead, the student performs a circular pattern in an abrupt way.

Remember: Symbols mean movement. The movement is sustained until the symbol ends.

A Crossing Side Step. To step across the body to the opposite side means that the leg must cross in front or in back. The beginner tends to turn the hips in order to make this easier. But there should be a minimum of displacement in the hip and it should return to normal as soon as possible.

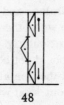

A Crossing Arm Gesture. When the arm is carried across the body into a gesture to the opposite side, it will normally flex slightly. For most people, performing the gesture with a normally straight arm would mean giving way in the body; i. e., turning a little in the chest. There should be as little of

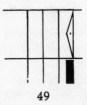

this as possible when the movement is supposed to be one of the arm alone. Naturally, flexibility in the shoulder area varies greatly with the individual; movement which can be performed with ease by one person may seem like comparative torture to another who must then make greater use of the body to compensate for his lack of flexibility.

A Backward Middle Arm Gesture. When the arm is lifted backward without any rotation, there comes a point at which the movement in the shoulder joint becomes restricted and the arm can only continue to move in space through the passive bending forward of the chest.

50a

If you start with the arm straight up and carry it backward without any rotation, there also comes a point at which the arm can no longer move.

50b

An Arm Circle. To negotiate a circle, the arm must rotate outward so that the shoulder is opened and hence made free. This opening of the shoulder we consider the natural way in which to perform smooth arm circles, and so it is not necessary to write the rotation. The body, particularly the rest of the chest, should not be affected. Movements of the arm alone should be distinct from what we call arm-and-body

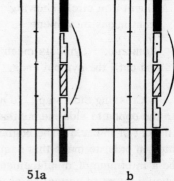

51a   b

movements in which the arm carries the body along so that it participates in the movement.

CHAPTER IV

Jumps, Open Positions of the Feet

SUPPORT AND ABSENCE OF SUPPORT

In the arm column a gap between symbols means an absence of movement. This is also true of the other gesture columns. In the support column, however, a gap between symbols means an absence of support.

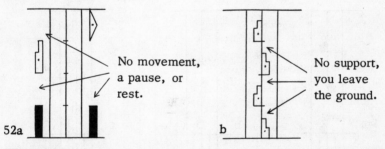

52a   No movement, a pause, or rest.

b   No support, you leave the ground.

The amount of space left between the symbols indicates how much the body rises from the ground. This may be very slight, or may extend over one or more beats.

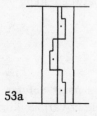

53a   Continuous steps, a normal walk.

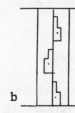

b   A simple run

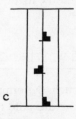

c   Leaps

In a normal walk the weight does not leave the ground at all between the transferences. In a run there is a small rising off the
ground, a releasing of the weight in between each step. In a leap
the body rises higher into the air and also uses a low support for
the take-off and landing. The length of the space between the support symbols shows the amount of time that you are in the air.
The longer the space the higher the jump, unless, of course, the
time in the air is being used to travel far rather than high, as in a
a long jump.

THE "HOLD WEIGHT" SIGN

To counteract this rule about leaving the ground, the "hold
weight" symbol is used. This sign is placed over one foot or over
both feet right after the previous support sign and lasts until it is
counteracted by another symbol. The following figure shows staccato steps, where the weight is held on the ground. In this way
variations in the rhythm and performance of steps can be indicated.

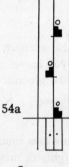
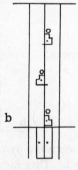
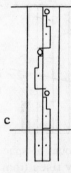

54a   b   c

| Staccato steps in low level | Staccato steps in middle level | Brief pause between steps |

THE WRITING CONVENTION

Through the simple convention of leaving the support column
blank, we are able to describe very directly the use of various kinds
of jumps. As in walking, even the simplest jump requires a coordinated use of the legs, knees, and feet. The less we spring off the

ground, the less we need to use the flexing action through the legs. To jump high, we must make full use of our "springboard." For general purposes we do not indicate all these details, but merely show by the amount of time that we are in the air the kind of preparatory movement required.

TYPES OF JUMPS

Note: We are here using "jumps" as a generic term referring to all modes of unsupported movement; i.e., to steps that take you into the air.

The Two General Categories. For purposes of notation, jumps fall into two general groups:

1. Simple, unadorned steps, such as are used in folk dancing, in which the various jumps are introduced in order to mark or accentuate the rhythms.

55a

2. Jumps in which the use of the legs in the air is of particular importance. For instance, jumps in which the legs are spread or the knees pulled up. In such cases, it is necessary to state what the legs do, and so the simple rule of merely leaving a space between the supports does not suffice. For these jumps, we must write two leg gestures. If you make gestures with both legs, you will be without a support, and so we come to the:

55b

Basic Rule Regarding Jumps:

A jump is written by leaving a space between support symbols, or by indicating two leg gestures. One leg gesture does not take you off the ground.

Capsule Rule: Two leg gestures or none:
            Double or nothing!

The Five Basic Forms. Any kind of aerial step, no matter how complicated, belongs to one of five basic forms. If you learn to recognize these at a glance, analyzing the more complex types becomes much easier later on.

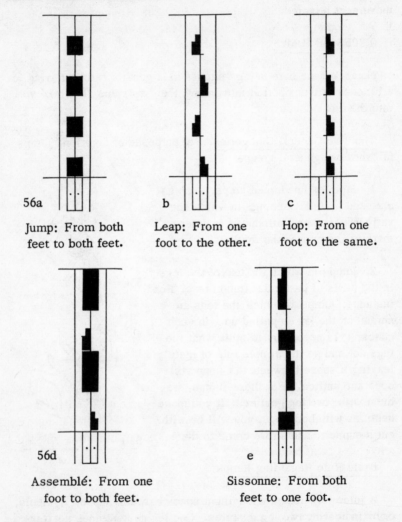

56a

Jump: From both
feet to both feet.

b

Leap: From one
foot to the other.

c

Hop: From one
foot to the same.

56d

Assemblé: From one
foot to both feet.

e

Sissonne: From both
feet to one foot.

Note: The terms assemblé and sissonne are seldom used outside of ballet, but the steps are found in all forms of dance, so you will recognize them whether or not you are familiar with ballet terminology.

OPEN POSITIONS OF THE FEET

In Chapter III, we introduced the closed positions of the feet, those in which your supports are directly underneath your center of weight but in which there were differences in the relationships of the legs to one another. The open positions, second and fourth, are those in which your center of weight is not over either support but is directly in between them. In the diagrams below, × marks the center of weight.

SECOND POSITION

57a

FOURTH POSITION

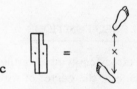

57b

Open 4th Position
(4th ouverte)

c

4th (or 6th) Position
(4th en avant)

Depending on the individual's training and source of information, the fourth position may be given different names. In notation we write movement itself and so are able to dispense with names. For general information, however, the names most frequently encountered have been indicated.

It is also possible to do a fourth position in which the exact center forward and back directions are used.   57d

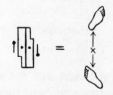

4th position croisée

The examples illustrated have been written for the right foot in front. The same can also be done for the left foot in front. In these figures a comfortable amount of turnout has been shown for the feet. As indicated previously, the support is the same and the level is the same whether you employ an outward rotation or not. We suggest that you perform these movements according to your natural degree of rotation.

The open positions can also be narrow or wide, in the same way that steps can be short or long. The pre-sign, placed between the two symbols, describes the distance of the support from your center.

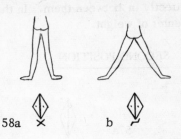

58a   b

TRAVELING JUMPS

CLOSED POSITIONS

A direction symbol in the support column indicates the traveling in space of the center of weight. Below are examples that have been covered so far.

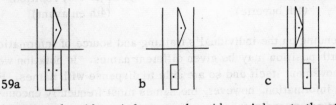

59a   b   c

A step to the side. The center of weight moves to the side.

A leap to the side. The center of weight moves to the side.

A leap to the other foot. The center of weight moves in the same way as in (a) and (b).

If you start with the feet together; that is, your support is in place, then you will travel the same amount if you land on one foot or the other, or on both.

60a	b	c
Landing on the right. Center travels to the right.	Landing on the left foot. Center travels to the right, as in (a).	Landing on both feet, a combination of (a) and (b). Center travels in the same way.

As long as your supports are underneath you, in place, any traveling in space from which you land on both feet can be written by using the direction symbols as in Fig. 60 (c). Thus, jumps in first, third, or fifth position can be written this way. This is because your supports travel in the same way as your center of weight; the two move as a unit.

OPEN POSITIONS

When you jump from a closed into an open position, your supports travel out from your center. Because each exerts an equal pull, your center does not move in space at all.

61a	b	c
Your center moves to the right.	Your center moves to the left.	Your center does not move; only the supports move away from your center.

Remember: Directions for supports are taken from your center, not from where a support was before.

In simple jumps in open positions, the support column is used to show the relation of your supports to your center. But if you are going to travel while jumping in open positions, this extra factor must be shown by an additional sign.

WAY SIGNS

A way sign to show the traveling of the center
of weight is placed outside the staff on the right,
adjacent to the jump it describes. Traveling on
a straight path is shown by short horizontal lines
connected as shown to the right. The direction of
the traveling is shown inside the broken vertical
line. This direction indicator is left blank since
there is usually no need to show level. 62

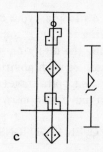

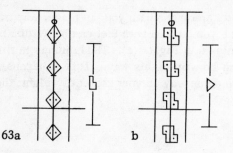

| Jumps in second position traveling forward. | Jumps in fourth position traveling to the right | The use of space can be indicated by the symbols × and ⌐. |

STEPPING INTO OPEN POSITIONS

Open positions present a problem because, as we have seen, your
center of weight (place) is not over your supports. This problem
comes up in stepping into open positions and in stepping from open
positions into closed ones. In an ordinary step, the weight is completely transferred from one foot to the other. When you step into
an open position, say second position, half of the weight is transferred to the foot that steps out and half is kept on the other foot.

The hold weight sign is used to
show that the weight is held on the
left foot. If there is also a change
of level, it must be shown by a
direction symbol, since the hold
sign does not indicate this. 64

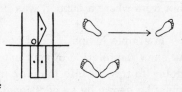

POSITION WRITING

In order to reach a position, we must first move into that position. If the manner in which we reach that position is important, then we must describe in detail the movement used. If, however, the main thing is to reach a position without much fuss, then it is better to state the position immediately and give just a general indication of how it is to be reached.

In Labanotation we introduce first the most direct way in which to describe the action, and leave for later the more careful analysis of the actual movement sequence that takes place.

We call this method "position writing," since the symbols describe the final position reached and not the movement which produces that position. A staple-like device is used to indicate how that position is reached.

To move from first position into second, using a change of level:

Starting Position: Destination:

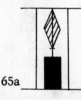   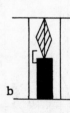

65a	b	c
Spring into 2nd, both feet move out equally.	Left foot remains where it is, right foot steps out.	Right foot remains where it is, left foot steps out.

The symbol [acts like a staple anchoring the foot to the ground, thus indicating that the position is reached by moving the other foot. The examples above show the three common ways of moving from one position into another. The staple is also used to indicate moving from an open position into a closed one, by being placed next to the foot which does not move.

STUDY IN SIMPLE JUMPS

Suggested music: "Country Gardens."

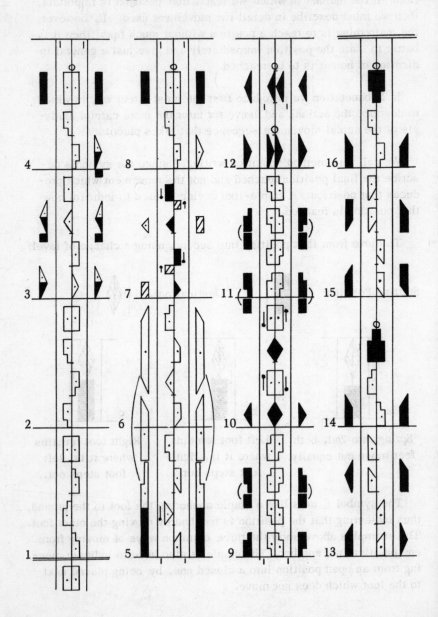

CLARIFICATIONS

LEVELS OF JUMPS

The levels of supports used in steps can also be used in writing jumps.

Middle Level

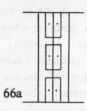

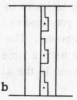

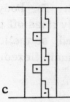

Slight springs in
first position

Hops in middle
level

A tiny spring before
each catch step

In all the above examples the body rises hardly at all into the air so there is only a little flexing through the feet, ankles and knees. Remember: middle level means in a horizontal plane; it does not indicate a stiff-kneed performance.

High Level

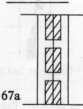

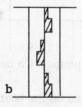

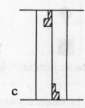

Tiny springs in first.
The rise from the
ground is achieved
mainly through the
use of the foot.

A tiny spring be-
tween each step,
a run in high level.
The knees flex
only a little.

This is wrong. Rising
off the ground for a
longer period requires
a low preparation and
a low landing.

The space between the supports indicates the time spent in the air. A high jump cannot be achieved from a high support; an adequate preparation must be indicated.

Low Level

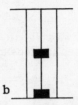

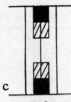

Tiny springs in low level. The body hardly rises off the ground, so the legs remain flexed.

High springs. More time is spent in the air, you land in order to rebound. The legs have ample time to extend in the air.

The actual use of levels in the process of a jump is shown above. However, this is usually taken for granted and not generally shown.

USE OF SPACE

It is important to know where to put the space which indicates going into the air. To land on the beat, you must be in the air just before the beat.

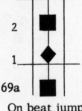

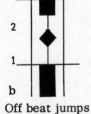

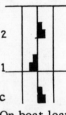

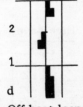

On beat jumps   Off beat jumps   On beat leaps   Off beat leaps

It is more common to land on the beat than it is to land off the beat. However, for syncopation or other rhythmic purposes, the accent may be in the air.

Watch out for the difference between a step, hop, and a leap, hop.

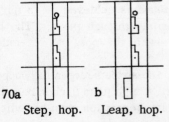

Step, hop.   Leap, hop.

EVEN AND UNEVEN RHYTHMS

In the examples below note the use of space to produce even and uneven rhythms in the same spatial patterns.

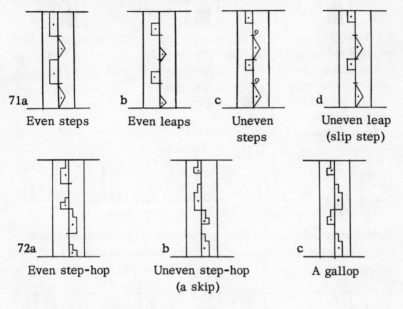

71a Even steps   b Even leaps   c Uneven   d Uneven leap
                                           steps   (slip step)

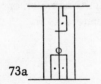

72a Even step-hop   b Uneven step-hop   c A gallop
                            (a skip)

THE HOLD WEIGHT SIGN

Duration and Cancellation. A hold weight sign lasts until something counteracts it. This may be another step, a leg gesture, or a straight line representing a leg gesture. The last is used when no movement in a direction is intended for the legs; they are in place, beneath your center of weight but not supporting it.

73a A step cancels   b The hold sign   c To hold the weight on the
     a previous   is cancelled   third count and step into
     hold sign.   by a step on   fourth position, the hold
                           count three.   sign must be repeated.

74a A hold sign is counteracted by specific leg gestures which show that you leave the ground.

b If no specific leg gestures are required, lines in the gesture columns indicate you go into the air.

c If leaving the ground is not indicated, just a step will occur on count three.

Some Incorrect Uses

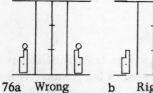 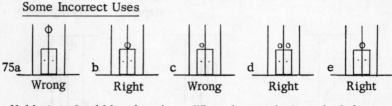

75a Wrong **b** Right **c** Wrong **d** Right **e** Right

Hold sign should be placed right after symbol.

When the weight is on both feet, the hold sign should be placed over both feet.

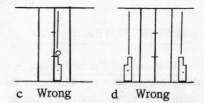

76a Wrong **b** Right **c** Wrong **d** Wrong

A hold sign is not needed for arm gestures. They remain where they are until another movement is written for them.

A line is not needed to show how long a hold sign or a position is held. It remains until some other movement counteracts it.

WAY SIGNS

Whenever you land on a single support, the direction into which you have traveled can be shown by a direction symbol for that support. But when you land with a divided support (feet apart), you need to show by an additional means the direction in space into

which the body traveled. Here is a little ditty to help you remember
when to use the way sign: The support column is busy,
> So you must show
> By means of a way sign
> Just where to go.

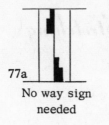

77a No way sign
needed

b No way sign
needed

c Step, jump
into second.

d A way sign is
needed to show
that the jump is
done traveling.

Remember: The traveling takes
place while you are in the air, so
that if only one jump is indicated
the way sign should be written for
the space of that one jump only.

78a Right

b Wrong

Direction is taken from your
center, not from where the support (foot) was previously. Thus,
in the two examples shown to the
right, you end up with both feet
together.

79a

b

OPEN POSITIONS: CORRECT PERFORMANCE

In open positions, the weight should
be placed equally on both feet. In performing the sequences, there is often a
tendency to favor one leg or the other, or
to raise the heels when they should be on
the ground. If two different levels are indicated in an open position, the center of
weight is nearer to the lower support.

Center of weight
is closer to the
80 right support.

CHAPTER V

Leg Gestures, Flexing and Stretching

LEG GESTURES

There is nothing very complicated about leg gestures; the legs move very much like the arms so far as direction and level are concerned; their scope, however, is more limited.

Occasionally the focus of a movement is on the leg gestures, but by and large it can be said that they are used to embellish other simple forms. This is particularly true of the different types of jumps, all of which can change character greatly through the use of different gestures. Since the classical ballet has specialized in this use of leg gestures, we will draw many of our examples from ballet.

The first examples make use of simple, whole leg gestures, without any bending or break in the knee joint. These forms can be further varied by employing flexed gestures as well as by combinations of flexing and straightening.

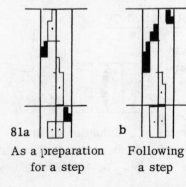 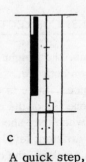 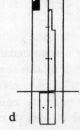

81a As a preparation for a step

b Following a step

c A quick step, slow gesture.

d A slow step, quick gesture.

TIMING OF LEG GESTURES

<u>During Steps.</u> As long as it is carrying weight, a leg is not free to make a gesture. This is a simple statement to which all will agree, and yet in writing movement we are often not aware of the precise moment when a transference of weight is completed and the leg is free to begin its gesture. This is particularly true in steps which are followed by fluent leg gestures.

The example at the right shows a step forward on the right leg, starting on the count of one and finishing on the count of two. At the same time, the left leg is performing a gesture forward, starting on the count of one and finishing on the count of two. Each of these movements can be performed separately, but they cannot be performed together. The left leg cannot start to gesture until it is free of weight, and - according to the symbol for the right leg - the transference of weight is not completed until the end of count two. The movement that was probably intended is shown in Fig. (b) where a slight overlap in movement shows the fluent transition. According to the analysis of a step, as given in Chapter II, this slight overlap is possible, but more than this would be a misstatement.

Wrong
82a

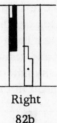

Right
82b

A change of weight and a leg gesture can occur together only if the movement is extremely fast. An instance of this is the coupé, a quick motion in which one leg is replaced by the other as the standing support.

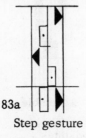

83a
Step gesture

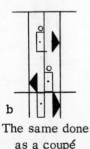

b
The same done
as a coupé

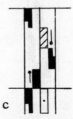

c
Step gesture

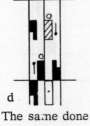

d
The same done
as a coupé

During Jumps: Two leg gestures cause you to leave the ground. If both legs perform gestures, your weight is on neither, and so you must go into the air. In order to go into the air after one gesture has been written, you must write the other. That is, jumps are shown by two leg gestures or none at all.

Remember: Double or Nothing!

You should become aware, as soon as possible, of the time relationship of leg gestures during jumps. Do the two gestures start simultaneously or does one precede the other?

As a general rule, it is safe to say that when you leave the ground from one foot, as in a leap, hop, and assemblé, the gesture of the free leg starts before you actually rise off the ground. When you leave the ground from both feet, the gestures begin simultaneously though one may last longer than the other, that is, continue to move after the other has ceased. This occurs in sissonnes when the leg on which you do not land continues its gesture after the landing has been made. In jumps - that is, leaving the ground from both feet and returning to both feet - the leg gestures are almost invariably symmetrical or parallel. These rules are the result of the natural need in the body for balance and for the change of weight.

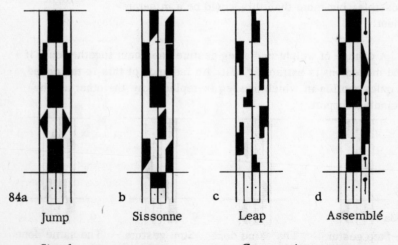

84a   b   c   d

Jump   Sissonne   Leap   Assemblé

Simultaneous gestures   Consecutive gestures

VARIATIONS IN THE USE OF LEG GESTURES

Note the differences in movement between the following:

85a No special gestures. The legs move out naturally to the open support.

b The legs remain under you, spreading just in time to take the open position.

c The legs spread immediately in the air and so are ready for the open position.

Note the differences in performing the following step-hop sequences:

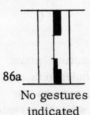 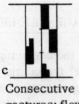

86a No gestures indicated

b One important gesture stated

c Consecutive gestures; flowing movement.

Note the differences in performance of these leaps:

87a A fluent leap with gestures

b A stilted leap

c A fast, split leap, suspended in the air. Note the absence of movement after the gestures.

Note: Most preparations for jumps are fast. A slow preparation produces a heavy movement.

CONTACT OF THE LEGS

Any contact between two parts of the body is shown by a connecting bow. This pictorially joins the two parts and indicates touching.

In ballet, the legs are often held together during a jump or sissonne, and for all beating movements, of course, they are brought together quickly.

88a Legs touch in the air

b Legs touch before opening

c Entrechat quatre

d Cabriole

PLACE MIDDLE FOR GESTURES

As the beginning student soon discovers, the direction "place middle" for an arm or leg gesture does not exist. In order to do such a thing one would have to have telescopic limbs, rather like the neck of a turtle. However, now that you are familiar with the correct use of the directions, we may present the use of place middle for movements in which you want to draw the limb in close to the body. This is usually done in order to extend the limb out into space again, so that place middle then becomes a direction through which you wish to pass, rather than an exact position in space. It cannot really be an exact position since our very use of it is in the nature of a convention. The drawing in of the limb toward the body may result in variances in movement when done by different individuals. It is, therefore, a generalization and is not used for exact or specific writing of gestures.

Typical examples for the arms and legs

89a b c

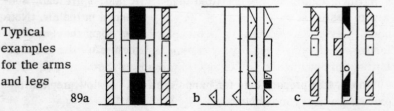

FLEXED AND STRETCHED LEGS

Normally the leg is held straight, with a relaxed knee. The foot is used as an extension of the leg, but is not stretched or taut. Such simple leg gestures, without any addition of style, are used in most folk dances.

STRETCHING THE LEG

The symbol for stretch is: ⌐ . This is the same symbol used for long steps. The basic idea is the same; that is, the symbol describes the use of space - long, far - which produces a long step or an extended limb.

A stretched leg gesture means that the knee is taut and the foot is extended. This use of the leg is a fundamental part of classical ballet and should appear in the key signature (similar to a key signature as used in music) to any ballet piece.

90a

A double stretched leg gesture, a further extension into space, means that the leg reaches out from the body, carrying the hip along with it.

90b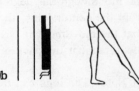

FLEXING (BENDING) THE LEG

The basic symbols for flexing are ✕ and ✳ . These are the same symbols used to describe small steps. Here, again, the idea is the same; that is, a small use of space. If your limbs are close to your body, they are not occupying as much space as when they are extended. By flexing your arm, you make it smaller. There is more latitude in bending the limbs than in stretching them, and so there are six degrees of flexing, each having its own variation of the basic symbols.

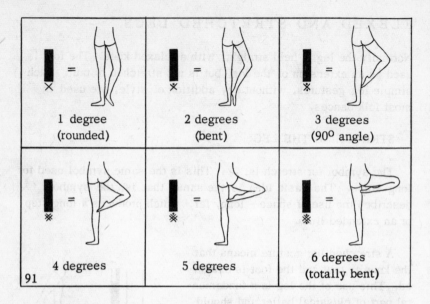

1 degree
(rounded)

2 degrees
(bent)

3 degrees
(90° angle)

4 degrees

5 degrees

6 degrees
(totally bent)

91

In these examples, the direction shown for the whole leg has been place low; that is, straight down. Though the leg flexes more and more, its extremities - the hip and the foot - maintain the same relationship with regard to level. In this case the foot remains below the hip though the degree of separation is varied. The limb bends from the center joint, the knee. The important thing to remember is that the movement is written in terms of the whole leg and not of the displacement in space of the knee which is incidental.

Note: The legs can flex and extend while supporting. The symbol for flex or extend is placed in the leg gesture column, since it describes the use of the leg as a limb and not as a support. Note the difference in meaning when the symbols × and ⌐ are used in the support column and in the leg gesture column.

92a

Short steps;
taut knees.

b

Long steps;
taut knees.

c

Short steps;
flexed knees.

d

Long steps;
flexed knees.

FLEXED AND STRETCHED ARMS

Normally the arm is held with a soft elbow and a relaxed (but not limp) wrist. The arms flex and stretch much as the legs do, using the same symbols.

STRETCHING THE ARM

A stretched arm gesture means that the arm is straight; the elbow, wrist, and hand are in a straight line. The fingers are straightened as part of the hand but are not especially taut or extended.

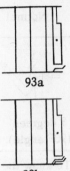

93a

A double stretched arm gesture - extending the arm farther out into space - means that the shoulder area is affected and moves as part of the arm, though this pulling out of the shoulder is not a large enough movement to cause displacement in space of the chest or torso.

93b

FLEXING (BENDING) THE ARM

The whole arm flexes in the same way as the whole leg. The extremities, the hand and the shoulder, keep the same space relation, and the limb bends from the center joint, the elbow:

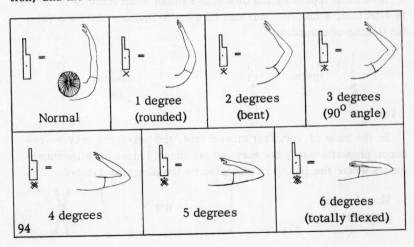

| Normal | 1 degree (rounded) | 2 degrees (bent) | 3 degrees (90° angle) |

| 4 degrees | 5 degrees | 6 degrees (totally flexed) |

94

If this forward arm gesture is done with the palm facing up, (that is, with an outward rotation), the degrees of flexing will be the same, but the result in space will be different because of the rotation:

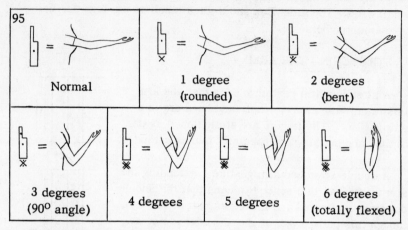

To know the exact position or movement in space while flexing, it is also necessary to know whether any rotation is employed, but this exactness is often not desired. In using these symbols the emphasis is on the flexing of the limbs rather than on their destination in space.

THE DURATION LINE

Instead of repeating the direction symbol when there is no change in direction, a duration line can be used to indicate the time value for flexing or extending.

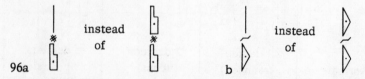

In the case of very fast movements, the pre-signs may be reduced proportionately but they are not drawn longer for slow movements where the length is indicated by the direction symbol.

STUDY IN LEG GESTURES

Suggested music: "The Irish Washerwoman" jig.

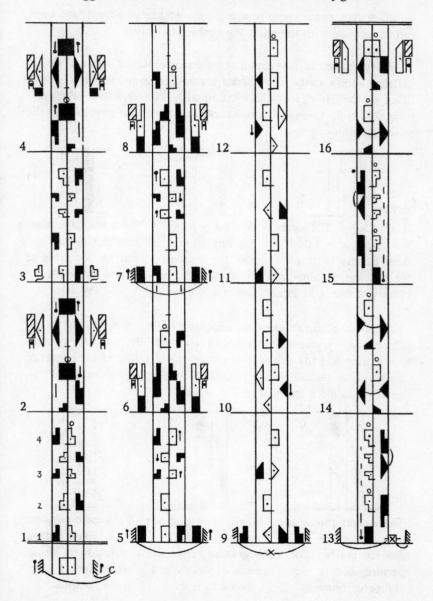

CLARIFICATIONS

THE STEP-GESTURE RULE

Rule: You cannot step (make a transference of weight) and perform a gesture with the other leg at the same time.

Every student of movement notation understands this and yet invariably shows these movements occurring simultaneously. What looks as though it is so and what actually is so are two different things. Let us re-examine this problem, which we have briefly discussed earlier.

98a A slow step. The symbol tells us to take three counts to transfer the weight completely to the right foot.

b A slow gesture. Starting on one, the leg reaches its destination at the end of three.

c Here we have these two movements written as occurring at the same time. Try it!

When you study an example such as Fig. (c), you can guess that a fluent step-gesture transition was intended. But it could not have been written had the writer been aware of the action of the center of gravity. Note the difference in performance in the examples below. Fig. 99 (b) is more fluent than Fig. 99 (a).

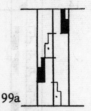

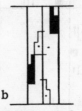

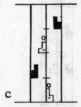

99a The weight comes to rest before the leg gesture starts. The performance is not staccato, however.

b The slight overlap indicates the start of the gesture before the center of weight has come to rest.

c A staccato performance. Each action is followed by a pause before the next begins.

The quicker the movement, the more it appears to the eye that the step and the gesture occur simultaneously. However, in order to perform them simultaneously, the weight of the body must be taken off the ground for a moment, and then it is possible to extend the one leg forward to its new support at the same moment that the other leg gestures backward. Note the exception to this rule on page 67, the coupé, in which the weight of the body remains in place.

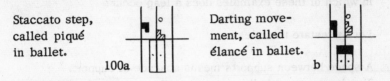

Staccato step, called piqué in ballet.

100a

Darting movement, called élancé in ballet.

b

Remember the slogan - First you step, and then you kick,
Unless you jump into it, quick!

Exception. A new support and a gesture can occur simultaneously after any aerial movement, as follows:

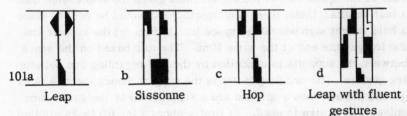

101a   b   c   d

Leap   Sissonne   Hop   Leap with fluent
gestures

Change of Level during a Gesture. A change of level on the supporting leg is not the same as a step - a transference of weight - and so it is, of course, quite possible to change level while gesturing with the other leg.

102

OCCURRENCE OF AERIAL MOVEMENTS: QUESTIONABLE EXAMPLES

The examples following give rise to doubts as to whether an aerial movement is intended or not. What is the rule when an empty space appears after a leg gesture? What if a support and a leg gesture end at the same time? When is it necessary to use a hold sign and when not?

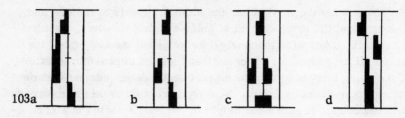

In which of these examples does a leap occur?

Let us restate the rules:

A space between supports means absence of support.
Two leg gestures indicate a jump. One leg gesture does not
cause you to leave the ground.

Following these rules, we find that there is no leaving the ground
in Fig. (a). There would also be no leap in Fig. (b), though the presence of the space across the leg columns gives the impression that
a leap occurs. Under these circumstances it would be best to place
a hold weight sign where the space is. In Fig. (c) the support and
the leg gesture end at the same time. The rule based on the space
between the supports is cancelled by the rule regarding one definite
leg gesture. The deciding factor is the support, hence the rule is to
go into the air when a gesture and a support end at the same time
unless a hold sign is used. At first glance, Fig. (d) looks similar
to (a) and no aerial movement would be expected, but study reveals
that the supporting leg is the one that gestures, hence a leap occurs
here.

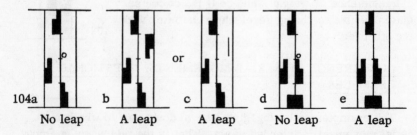

In order to go into the air in Fig. 104 (a), the second leg gesture
must be written. If no particular direction is to be indicated for
this gesture, a straight line in the leg gesture column can be used.

RELATIVE DIRECTION VERSUS ABSOLUTE DIRECTION

Many people fall into the mistake of judging the direction of a movement according to where the limb previously was in space, relating the path of movement to that position rather than describing the absolute directions around the body. To make this clear, let us take a typical example.

As a starting position, the right leg is gesturing backward low. We want to bring this leg next to the left leg. The direction to which the leg moves is place. This is the absolute direction. The relative direction of the movement is forward but not forward of the body.

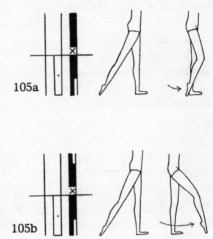

105a

Note the difference in performance when a forward symbol is written, as in Fig. (b).

105b

INCORRECT WRITING OF AN ASSEMBLÉ

In an assemblé you leave the ground from one support and land on both. The leg gestures that occur during an assemblé are not simultaneous but consecutive. Note the difference in the examples to the right.

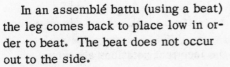

106a   Wrong   b   Right

In an assemblé battu (using a beat) the leg comes back to place low in order to beat. The beat does not occur out to the side.

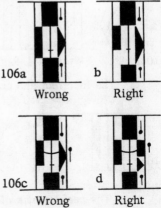

106c   Wrong   d   Right

INCORRECT PERFORMANCE: BENDING THE ARMS

The execution of flexing arm movements is not always correct. The tendency is to move only the lower arm, instead of performing a flexing movement in the whole limb.

Starting with the arm up, the whole arm should flex, causing a movement in the shoulder joint as well as the elbow.

Starting with the arm down, the whole arm draws in toward the center; that is, the shoulder area.

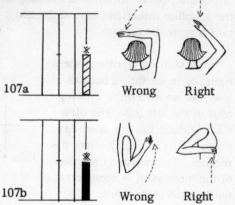

107a   Wrong   Right

107b   Wrong   Right

INCORRECT WRITING: BENDING THE LEGS

The most common error here is in writing rather than in reading. The positions shown below are often written with the incorrect direction symbol because the writer is thinking in terms of where the knee moves in space, rather than seeing the movement as one of the leg as a whole and noting the relation between its extremities - the foot and the hip.

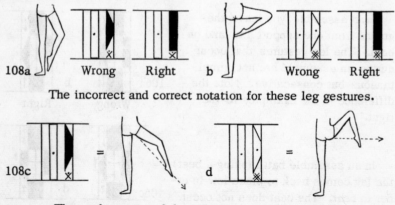

108a   Wrong   Right   b   Wrong   Right

The incorrect and correct notation for these leg gestures.

108c   =   d   =

The performance of the incorrect notations above.

CHAPTER VI

Circular Path, Turns,
Use of Body and Space Holds

STAGE DIRECTION INDICATORS

So far, though we have discussed moving in various directions, we have not considered turning our facing direction away from the front of the room (the audience). In many cases, however, and on the stage especially, changes in the direction into which you are facing are most important.

To describe this, we use white pins to represent the fixed stage directions. Thus, ⓣ means facing the front, the audience; ⍤— means facing stage right; ⍭ means facing upstage, or with the back to the audience. The various diagonal directions are written in the same manner. These pins are used to indicate the starting position in a movement sequence and are used subsequently whenever necessary to clarify a change in direction. They are written on the left of the staff, on the outside, where they can be seen clearly.

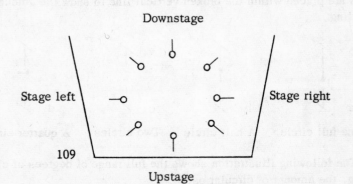

Downstage

Stage left   Stage right

Upstage

CIRCULAR PATH

In Chapter IV we explored a few of the possibilities of traveling on a straight path. This path, you will recall, is written alongside the jumps or other movements which are performed while traveling. It is also possible to travel on curved or circular paths. The most familiar form of this is walking in a circle.

To show a curved path, the straight way sign is modified. The lines at the beginning and end are slanted to show the direction of the curve, clockwise or counterclockwise.

DIRECTION OF CIRCLING
_____

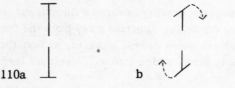

110a   Straight way sign

b   Circling to the right, clockwise.

c   Circling to the left, counterclockwise.

(The dotted lines are merely for clarification.)

AMOUNT OF CIRCLING
_____

In addition to indicating the way of circling, we must state clearly how much of a circle is to be performed. As indication, black pins are placed within the broken vertical line to show the amount of circling.

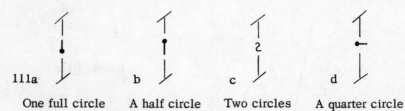

111a   One full circle

b   A half circle

c   Two circles

d   A quarter circle

The following illustration shows the full range of degrees of circling, the amount of circular path.

DEGREES OF CIRCLING

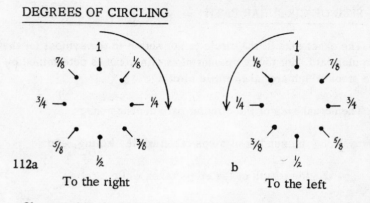

112a **To the right**

b **To the left**

Observe that the black pins are used for two purposes: to indicate the relationship of two parts - when placed next to a direction symbol - and to indicate degree of circling when placed within a circular path or turn sign. Do not confuse the use of these black pins with that of the white pins which describe the fixed directions on stage.

The diagram to the right represents a path walked with forward steps. This path can be broken up into portions of circling: 1/4 circle clockwise; 1/2 circle counterclockwise; straight for a few steps; 1/4 circle counterclockwise; 3/4 circle clockwise. Below is the notation for this path in space.

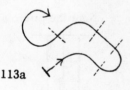

113a

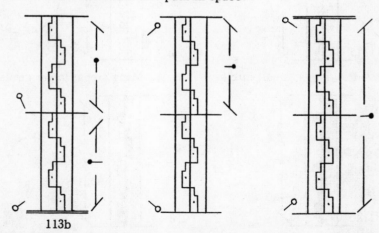

113b

Note: The sign for circling is placed on the right of the staff.

SIZE OF CIRCULAR PATH

The exact size of the circle is not shown in the symbol for the circular path, nor in the amount of circling, but is determined by the steps which are taken while circling.

The actual size of the circular path depends on:

    1. the number of steps taken while circling, and

    2. the length of the steps taken while circling.

The fewer the steps, the smaller the circle performed.
The smaller the steps, the smaller the circle performed.

Thus, the actual path on the floor is determined by the steps taken. If the steps are all in place, you will merely circle around yourself without moving out into space at all.

Note the difference in the examples below:

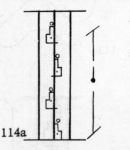

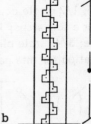

114a   Few steps; small circle.   b   Many steps; larger circle.

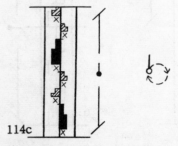

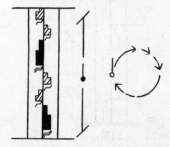

114c   Small steps; small circle.   d   Longer steps; larger circle.

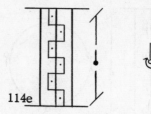

114e

f

Absence of directional steps
means no path - circling in
place. The result is turning
around oneself.

Less amount of circling; a
quarter of a circle arc.

SITUATION OF THE CIRCLE

Many variations of walking circles are possible. The simplest
ones to understand and the most common are those in which forward
steps are used. It is also possible, however, to circle while walking backwards or taking sideward steps. In these instances the problems are: Where does the circle lie in relation to the performer when
backward or sideward steps are taken? Which way is clockwise and
which is counterclockwise?

Forward Steps. When taking forward steps, the center of the circle lies to your right when you travel clockwise and to your left
when you travel counter-clockwise.

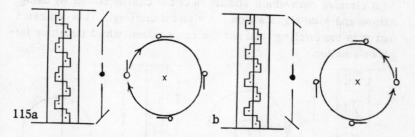

115a

b

Circle lies to right.

Circle lies to left.

Backward Steps. When taking backward steps, the center of the
circle lies to your left when you circle clockwise and to your right
when you circle counter-clockwise.

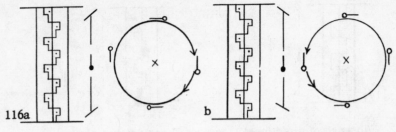

Circle lies to left.   Circle lies to right.

<u>Sideward Steps.</u> When you take sideward steps to the right, the center of the circle lies in back of you when you circle clockwise; in front of you when you circle counter-clockwise.

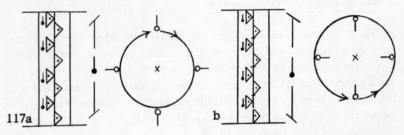

Circle lies in back.   Circle lies in front.

SPIRALS

A circular path which spirals in or out can be shown by using narrow and wide signs within the sign for circling. This indicates that it is the circling, and not the steps taken, which becomes larger or smaller.

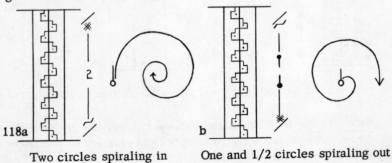

Two circles spiraling in   One and 1/2 circles spiraling out

STUDY IN CIRCULAR PATH

Suggested music: "La Comparsita" tango.

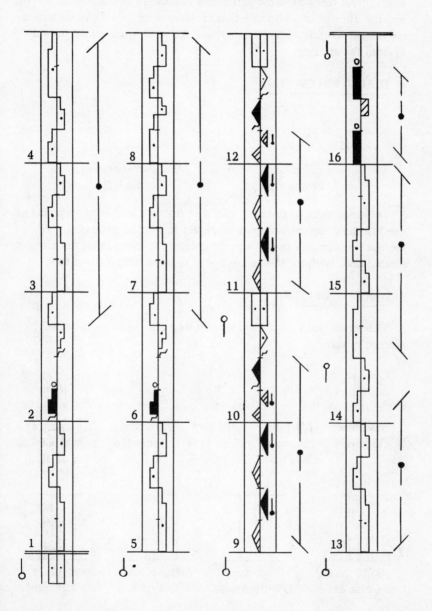

PIVOT TURNS

Closely related to circling is turning, or pivoting around one's own axis. Pivot turns are also performed clockwise or counterclockwise, and the amount of pivoting - that is, degree of turn - can be indicated within the turn sign. The symbol for turning is similar to the symbol for circling.

DIRECTION OF TURN

119

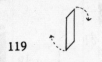

| Clockwise | Counterclockwise |
| (to the right) | (to the left) |

Different parts of the body can turn (rotate), and so the symbol is used in the different columns wherever turning is indicated. When the symbol appears in the support column, it means that the support rotates and, with it, the entire body, thus causing a pivot turn.

AMOUNT OF TURN

The same black pins used for circling are used to show the amount of turn.

120a   b   c   d   e

One turn	1/4 turn	3/4 turn	1/8 turn	As many as
clockwise	counter-	clockwise	clockwise	possible (sign
	clockwise			for ad lib.)

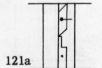

121a   b   c   d

| Step, turn | Step, turn | Step, pivot | Step, pivot |
| 1/4 clockwise. | 1/2 clockwise. | a full turn. | two full turns. |

LEVEL OF PIVOT TURNS

The turn sign does not indicate level. A turn is performed in
the same level as the previous step or support.

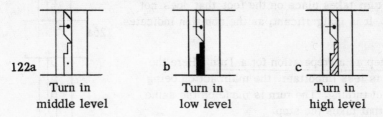

122a
Turn in
middle level

b
Turn in
low level

c
Turn in
high level

However, if there is a change in level, it can be shown in two
ways: by indicating the new level of the support and tying it to the
turn sign as in Fig. 123 (a) and (c) or by shading part of the turn sign
as in Fig. 123 (b) and (d).

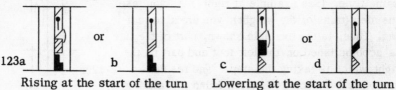

123a   b
Rising at the start of the turn

c   d
Lowering at the start of the turn

In a longer turn, a change in level can be shown as occurring at
the beginning, in the middle, or at the end of the turn. It is also
possible to show more than one change in level during a longer pivot.

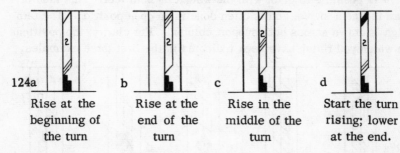

124a
Rise at the
beginning of
the turn

b
Rise at the
end of the
turn

c
Rise in the
middle of the
turn

d
Start the turn
rising; lower
at the end.

Note that in shading the turn sign to indicate
change in level, the basic shape of the parallelogram
is kept intact. As indicated here the shading follows
the angular lines at top and bottom of the turn sign.   125

COMBINATIONS OF STEP-TURN

Turn as a Preparation for a Step. This is usually done in order to face into a new direction. The turn takes place on the foot that does not step. It is insignificant, as the notation indicates.

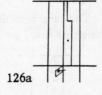

126a

Step as a Preparation for a Turn. Here the step is less important, the main action being that of turning. The turn is made on the same foot that takes the step.

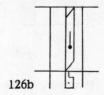

126b

Step and Turn Simultaneously. We tie the two symbols for step and turn together with a bow which shows that the two actions happen at the same time. (See example at right.) As you take the step (transfer the weight), you are also turning. Thus, in the example shown, part of the turn is accomplished on the left foot and part on the right which is taking the step. The result is a smooth curve such as is often found in waltzing.

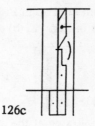

126c

PIVOT TURNS ON TWO FEET

It is possible to pivot with the weight on both feet. This kind of turn is like a swivel and is often done in an open position. The turn sign is drawn across both support columns. For clarity, the positions in which you finish have been indicated in the first three examples.

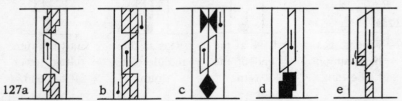

127a   b   c   d   e

Fig. (d) shows a turn starting on both feet and finishing on the right foot. In Fig. (e) the reverse occurs; the turn starts on the right foot, then the left is placed on the floor, and the turn continues on both feet.

TURNS IN THE AIR

A turn in the air is a turn of the whole body, but without the weight being supported on either leg. To indicate this, the turn sign is written over both support columns as with turns on both feet. However, the presence of leg gestures - indicated either with direction symbols or straight lines - shows that the body is in the air.

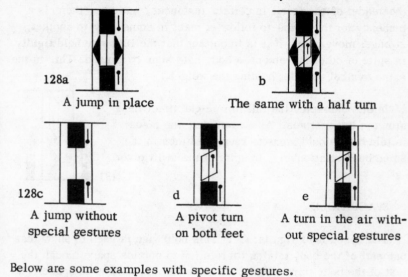

128a

A jump in place

b

The same with a half turn

128c

A jump without special gestures

d

A pivot turn on both feet

e

A turn in the air without special gestures

Below are some examples with specific gestures.

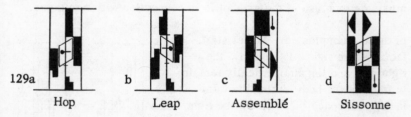

129a

Hop

b

Leap

c

Assemblé

d

Sissonne

As with turns on the floor, it is possible to start the turn on one foot and then to go into the air. It is also possible to start by turning in the air, to land, and to continue turning all the while.

Turn started on one foot, then into the air.

130a

Turn in the air, then on one foot.

b

USE OF BODY AND SPACE HOLDS

BODY HOLD

Normally a limb remains in the direction into which it last moved until it is given something new to do. This holding of parts of the body is understood, and it is not usually necessary to remind the reader of the fact. In certain instances, however, there is a tendency for the limbs to follow or react in some way to another, stronger movement. If it is important that the limbs be held rigidly, in spite of other movement, a body hold sign o is used. This is the same symbol used for holding the weight.

In this example, the full turn might affect the arm and leg gestures. As a reminder, the reader is told by the hold signs to keep the limbs in the same body relationship, in spite of the swift pivot.

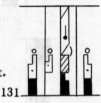

131

SPACE HOLD

The space hold sign is: ◇ . This hold sign is used to show that one part of the body retains its relation to outside space though the rest of the body turns away or changes its relationship to space. The most common use of the symbol is in connection with turn signs.

In these examples, the dancer starts facing stage right. In Fig. (a), the right arm and leg automatically remain in front of the body during the turn. In (b), the space holds cause the right arm and leg to hold their former room direction, while the rest of the body turns away. They will thus end in the position of backward gestures.

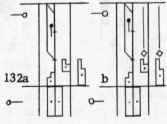

132a   b

Although the space hold sign is called a hold sign, it is not a hold from the point of view of movement in the body, and so it is treated as a movement sign. For this reason it is followed by a line to show the time value.

REVOLVING ON A STRAIGHT PATH

This is a simple form of movement which appears in many folk dances, in ballroom dancing, as well as in other more complex forms. To break down in detail the adjustments in space that occur during this movement is often unnecessary. It is best, therefore, not to describe it in terms of directional steps and pivot turns but rather to state the over-all result by making use of two forms of way signs.

Fig. 133 shows a series of steps followed by pivot turns. You start facing front and turn 1/8 on each step; you end up facing the opposite direction. You will then find that you have actually been walking on a straight line.

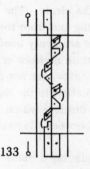

The notation of the pivot turns and the change in the direction of each step gives the impression that the sequence must be performed with great exactness. 133

In Fig. 134 the same space pattern is written, but an over-all description is used. First, the forward steps tell you to travel on a straight path into that direction. Secondly, the circling sign on the outside tells you to perform a half revolution during those steps. Thirdly, the encompassing straight lines at the beginning and end of the circling sign tell you to make not a circular but a straight path in space. Thus you circle around yourself while walking on a straight path. 134

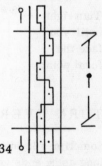

The advantages of writing revolving on a straight path can be seen when an uneven number of steps is used. In the example given above, the pattern can be broken down into degrees of pivot turns. But had five steps been taken to revolve a half turn, or seven, this breakdown into degrees of turn would have been awkward. Through using the revolving-on-a-straight-path sign all minute calculations are eliminated and it is up to the reader to proportion the movement so that smooth transitions are produced.

Revolving on a straight path is also called
a straightened-out-curved-path. As can be
seen from the diagram to the right, it is
the same pattern that is performed on a
curved path, but straightened out.   135

FOCAL POINT FOR CIRCLE DANCES

In circle dances, the chief orientation for each dancer is his relation
to the circle. The steps are done facing into the center of the circle,
facing out from the center of the circle, and so on. Stage direction
pins are rarely used since each person faces a different direction and
there is no front or back to a circle. Even the degrees of turn, 1/4,
1/2, etc., are not of as much value, though they can be used. Most
important is the dancer's relation to the focal point - the center of
the circle - which may lie in front, in back, to the right or left. The
in-between diagonal directions may also be used, but this is rarer.

By placing a black circle on the turn sign the following instructions
can be given:

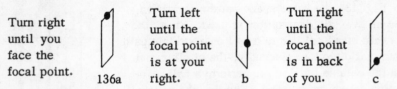

| Turn right until you face the focal point. 136a | Turn left until the focal point is at your right. b | Turn right until the focal point is in back of you. c |

TURN OVER RIGHT OR LEFT

Sometimes it does not matter whether a dancer turns right or left as
long as he ends up facing a certain direction. When a group has been
facing into different directions, it is often easiest to indicate that
everyone turns to face a particular stage direction; each individual
will turn right or left, whichever is easier and simpler for him. The
symbol is a combination of the two turn signs.

Turn over right
or left.   137a

Turn either way
to face the front
of the stage.   b

Turn either way
to face the focal
point.   c

STUDY IN TURNS

Suggested music: Triumphal March from "Aida"
(main theme).

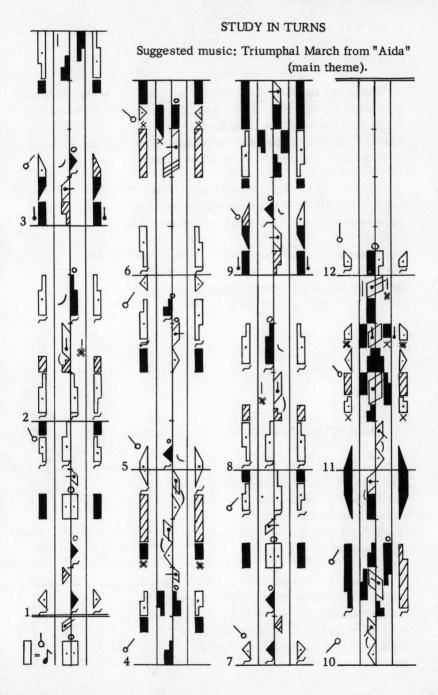

CLARIFICATIONS

TURNS

Distinction Between Black and White Pins. The white and black pins stand for two different things. The white pins represent the stage directions and are constant body directions in relation to space. The black pins describe the amount of turn and thus are relative space directions. Note the difference:

A full turn; end by facing where you are now. This does not tell you where you face on stage, but merely tells you to turn right until you face that direction again.

Turn right to face the audience. This does not tell you the amount of turn done in order to face front; this will depend on where you were facing previously.

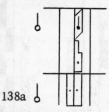

138a

One full turn that starts
and finishes facing front

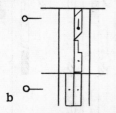

b

One full turn that starts
and finishes facing right

Turn on Supporting Leg. If a pivot turn is to be written on one foot, the weight must previously be shown to be on that foot. Note example (b) which is a possible interpretation of the ambiguous notation in Fig. 139(a).

139a Wrong   b Right

Fig. 140(a) poses the same problem; it could likewise be given several different interpretations. Fig. (b), however, indicates very clearly that the weight is taken over to the right foot in order to turn on that support.

140a   b

CHAPTER VII

Floor Plans, Drafting a Score,

Repeat Signs

By now you have learned to read and to write a rather large number
of basic movements. In fact, you are well able to write some simple pieces - certain folk dances, for example. Therefore, in this
chapter, we introduce methods of notating the use of stage space,
the indication of group formations, of entrances and exits, as well
as the planning of a score and the coordination of the movement notation with the stage diagrams. All the details included in this chapter are not necessary for a first venture but they will be useful for
later reference.

FLOOR PLANS

Floor plans show the dancers' positions and formations on stage
and how they change. In a complete dance score, these plans are
written beside the movement notation, wherever they are needed.
They can also be written on a separate sheet for the use of the director, since glancing over the floor plans is an easy way to get an
over-all idea of the pattern of the dance. The plans for the director
are written from his point of view; that is, as seen from the audience. Within the score, the plans are written from the dancer's
point of view; that is, facing the audience.

THE STAGE

The stage area, as drawn, shows the three walls and an open
side for the audience. Though stages vary in size, their shape is
fairly consistent.

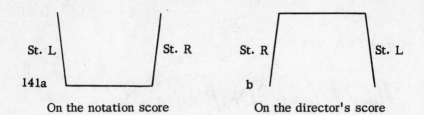

| On the notation score | On the director's score |

The group movement of the dancers can be specifically indicated or merely outlined. For a complete score, all the details should be written in. However, it is useful to know certain generalizations when notating floor plans quickly during rehearsals. In such cases, the notator may be able to get only the over-all pattern at first. Then as the work is done over again, he can fill in the details. For this reason, we will start with the general outline of group notation and become more specific as we go along.

GENERAL GROUPINGS

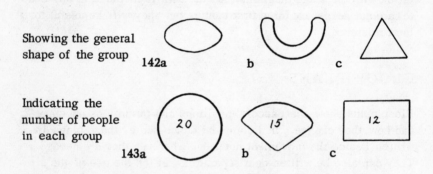

Showing the general shape of the group 142a   b   c

Indicating the number of people in each group 143a   b   c

Note: From now on, all diagrams are drawn from the dancer's point of view.

General Formations.

144a   Line (file) facing stage right, 4 people.   b   Line (file) facing the audience, 5 people.

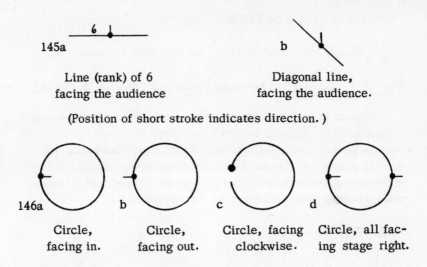

145a   Line (rank) of 6
        facing the audience

b   Diagonal line,
     facing the audience.

(Position of short stroke indicates direction.)

146a   Circle,
        facing in.

b   Circle,
     facing out.

c   Circle, facing
     clockwise.

d   Circle, all fac-
     ing stage right.

General Group Action. The over-all pattern of the group movement on stage can be shown by using arrows and lines.

The stage action roughly indicated
here shows a group of ten people
entering upstage-left and moving
across to the upstage-right corner.
A line of three people enter down-
stage-left and face the group in
the corner.

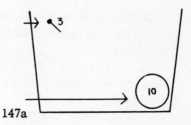

147a

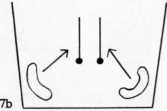

147b

Two curved formations move
downstage and center and
form two lines facing
the audience.

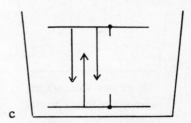

c

A few arrows indicate clearly
that the two lines, facing each
other, cross. The line moving
downstage passes through
the line moving upstage.

SPECIFIC STAGE NOTATION

To identify individual dancers, the following are used.

Boy ⊥   Girl ⊥   Alternate indicators: Boy ● ▲ Girl ○ △

The point of the pin indicates the direction into which the dancer is facing. The alternate indicators are used when two sets of pins need to be drawn on one plan, the straight ones illustrating the starting position of the dancers and the others the ending position. In this way, the reader does not get the impression that there are twice as many people on stage as they actually are.

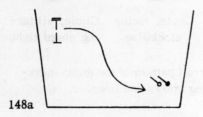

148a

The dancers start downstage
left and end upstage right.

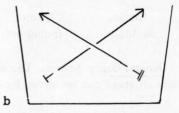

b

When two paths cross, the
broken line indicates that the
other dancer passes in front.

Note the two different uses of the arrow in relation to the pins.

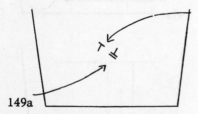

149a

The arrows indicate the
dancers' paths, showing
where they finish.

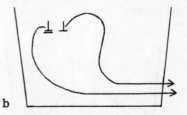

b

The arrows lead from the
dancers' position on stage
and show where they exit.

The formations shown previously can now be written more exactly. For example:

150a ●——4——— = ╢ ╟ ╢ ╟   b ——6●—— = ⊥⊥⊥⊥⊥⊥

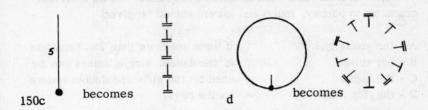

150c   becomes   d   becomes

Individual Identification. Letters of the alphabet are usually se-
lected to identify the individual dancers. The choice of letters will
depend on the type of dance. We will consider three main categories.

Partners. In group dances such as folk dances, where there are
partners who dance together most or all of the time, it is logical to
identify the dancers in couples.

A - a girl   MA - her partner   151a   MA A   MB B
B - a girl   MB - her partner

                        Partners   MA   B
                        have changed   151b   A   MB

Group or Corps. When the dancers work as a unit and have no individual significance, it is better to identify the group and to number the dancers in it.

Group A: A1 - (Mary)   Group B: B1 -   ⊥3 ⊥3
         A2 - (Ruth)   B2 -
         A3 -   B3 ·   ⊥2 ⊥2

                                              152a   ⊥1 ⊥1
                                                     A   B

Should the groups merge for a   A3 A2 ⊥   A1 ⊥ ⊥
while, more careful identification   T   T   B3 T   B2 B1
may be necessary.
                                          152b

Dance Drama. In a work in which each dancer has an individual character to portray, individual letters should be given.

A - the young girl

B - her suitor

C - the father

D - the rich duke

If there are more than 26 characters in the dance, single letters can be used for the girls and double letters for the boys.

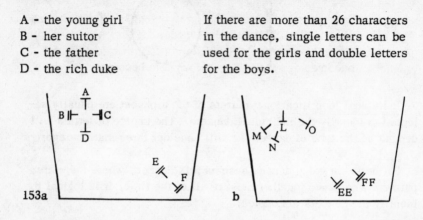

153a   b

Large Groups and Ensembles. The use of odd and even numbers is helpful to identify individuals in large groups which move in an orderly and symmetrical way. Some large ballets and ensembles, such as the Rockettes at Radio City Music Hall, use formations which require this means of identification. The stage left dancers are given odd numbers and their counterparts on stage right are given even numbers. The dancers in front are given the low numbers; those in the back will have the higher numbers. When groups mix together and later separate, it is then easy to see where the individuals belong, much as horses are numbered in the circus! In this type of ballet, the actual steps are simple, the dancer's problem being to find where she belongs and where she must go at each change in formation. This numbering system helps her to keep track of her place.

1 ⊥   ⊥ 2

3 ⊥   ⊥ 4

5 ⊥   ⊥ 6

7 ⊥   ⊥ 8

9 ⊥   ⊥ 10

154a   11 ⊥   ⊥ 12

A two-line formation

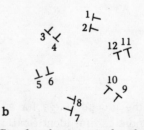

b

Couples form a circle, facing clockwise.

COORDINATION OF PLANS AND SCORE

On the notated score, the floor plans are placed on each page. To show exactly to which measure each plan belongs, the number of that measure is written next to the floor plan. Thus, even if a complete score is not written, the floor plans, coordinated with the music score, offer an excellent reminder of the action of the dance.

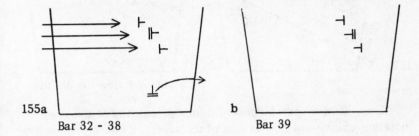

155a   Bar 32 - 38   b   Bar 39

The number of floor plans needed to clarify the action will depend on the number of people on stage, the use of the space, the overlapping of paths, and other similar factors. The use of colors is often employed when several crossing paths occur on one diagram.

SEQUENCE OF ACTION

Several paths can be written on one floor plan even though they are not performed simultaneously. The sequence of the action can be indicated by labeling the paths 1st, 2nd, 3rd.

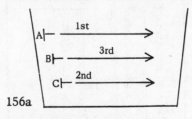

156a

A moves first; then C;
then B.

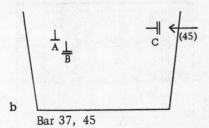

b   Bar 37, 45

This plan shows the position
for A and B on bar 37, and the
entrance of C on bar 45.

DESCRIPTION OF MOVEMENT

As a general guide, before the notated score has been made, word descriptions of the type of movements can be indicated on the floor plans.

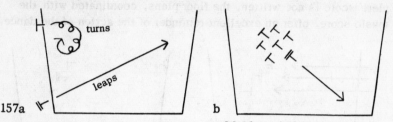

157a

b

Maidens follow the old man.

Note: This chapter purposely omits discussion of the group notation which is written as part of the score. Explanations on how to write canon form, holding or changing formations, following a leader, and the like, are given in a later chapter.

DRAFTING THE SCORE

The dance score is like the music score in that all the parts are joined together. The bar lines are extended across all the staves that are being used. The numbers of the bars are placed at the left. These correspond with the bars in the music score which have also been numbered for quick reference. A separate staff is used for each individual dancer. Only one staff, however, need be used for a group which moves in unison.

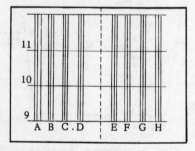

158a
Each dancer is given
a separate staff.

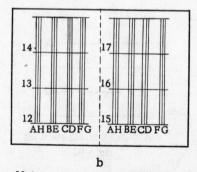

b
Unison in movement allows
for condensation of the score.

ARRANGEMENT OF DANCERS

Principals, soloists, or leading characters are given the staves at the left of the score; the groups are written on the right. When several people move alike for any length of time, the movement can be written on the same staff. However, if unison movement lasts for only a short time, it is not worth while to lump the staves together and then have to readjust them.

When a dancer on stage has no movement, a hold sign is placed at the bottom of his staff on each page. An empty staff without this hold sign indicates that the dancer is temporarily off stage. In the example to the right, B and C are on stage but inactive; D, G, and H are off stage.

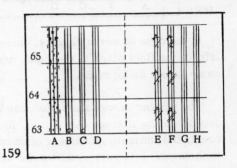

159

PLACEMENT OF THE FLOOR PLANS

To use the maximum amount of space on the page for two, four, or eight people, the score should be arranged as shown below.

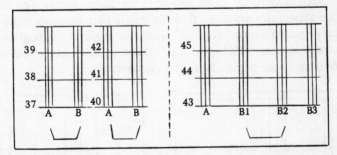

160

The floor plans are placed below the staves, each plan taking care of the measures above it. When necessary the exact measure of the plan can be stated.

In the case of five or six dancers, the following arrangement is better, where the floor plans are placed in the unused side area.

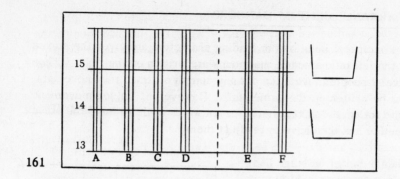

161

In the case of seven dancers, there is not really enough room left for the floor plans at the right, and so it is better to use the same layout as for eight.

The number of measures that can be placed on one page will depend on the timing. As a rule, four squares are taken for each count, but intricate movement often calls for six or eight squares to each count. It is very usual for the dance bars to coincide in size with the average size of the corresponding music bars.

COMBINATION OF DANCE AND MUSIC SCORE

The complete dance score should include the music. This is placed vertically to the extreme left of the dance score. The music must be especially drawn so that the music bars coincide with the regularly spaced dance bars. Allowance is made at the beginning for the key signature and the clefs. These appear next to the starting position at the beginning of the dance score.

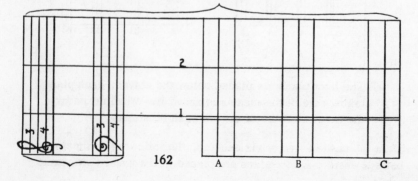

162

For general purposes, the music and dance scores are kept separate, the coordination between them being the identical numbering of the bars throughout. When music is included in a dance score, it is for the benefit of the dancer rather than the musician, hence the vertical rather than horizontal placement.

ENTRANCES AND EXITS

Entrances and exits are shown by double lines. The word "exit" is also used, and often a small stage plan to show which stage wing the dancer uses. In the example shown here, A exits and C enters; B has been on stage when the phrase starts and stays there. 163

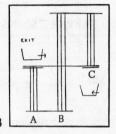

FLOOR PLAN PINS WRITTEN IN THE SCORE

The stage pins for men and women can also be used alongside the notation score in order to facilitate reading sequences in which the dancers' movements relate to one another. By seeing at a glance where they are facing in relation to each other, the dancers can read more easily any partnering actions that may follow.

In Fig. 164, A stands with her left hand grasping B's left hand. Her right hand is placed on his left shoulder. Because of the presence of the two stage pins, it is easy to ascertain just how this is done. This pattern could also have been done with the couple in this relationship: ⊢⊣

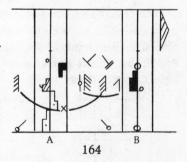

164

The placement on the notation score of these stage pins depends on the space available. When there is room they are written between the staves of the dancers whose positions they describe. They should be placed so that they do not interfere with the movement notation. It is important to give the right impression of the proximity of the two dancers; note the slight differences in relationship between the following: ⊢ ⊣   ⊢⊣   ⊥

REPEAT SIGNS

To facilitate writing, we make use of repeat signs. For the final
draft of a score, it is better to write out the repeats in full, however.
In some instances, repeats are easy to read, but they must be
avoided in cases where they add to the complexity of reconstruction.

REPEAT SIGNS PLACED WITHIN THE STAFF

165   ⫶∕⫶   Repeat the same
(identical repeat).   ⫶⫻⫶   Repeat to the
other side (sym-
metrical repeat).

An identical repeat is easily understood. A repeat to the other side,
as it is commonly called, means performing a symmetrical pattern,
using the opposite side of the body to move to the opposite side.

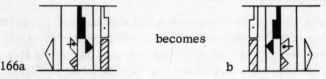

166a   becomes   b

This example shows a movement performed to the other side.

The repeat sign always refers back to the last written measure
or count, unless the number of another measure is indicated. It is
placed in the center of the area to which it refers. If the area is
small, the repeat sign is small. In the case of a whole bar, the
repeat sign is drawn larger.

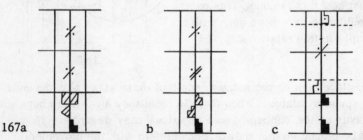

167a   b   c

If the repeat area does not coincide with the established bar, dotted
lines are drawn to indicate the repeated area. Thus, Fig. (c) shows
a 4-count repeat in a 3-count bar.

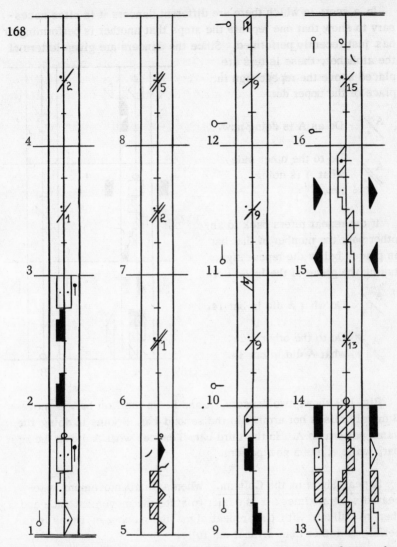

When a number is placed underneath the repeat sign, it refers to the measure to be repeated.   Slight changes in a repeat can be shown. The repeats of bar 9 show changes in the turn. Bar 14 has no steps, and there is no turn at the end of Bar 16.

As many repeats as possible were used in the sequence above.   For speed in reading it is desirable to write the movement out in full.

In a score in which there are different dancers it is often necessary to show that one repeats the steps that another is performing or has just recently performed.   Since the dancers are given letters of

the alphabet, these letters are placed above the repeat sign in place of the upper dot.

A⁄•   Do as A is doing now.

A⁄⁄•   Do to the other side what A is doing now.

If the repeat refers back to another bar, the number of that bar is placed below the repeat sign, taking the place of the lower dot.

A⁄14   Do what A did in bar 14.

A⁄⁄14   Do to the other side what A did in bar 14.

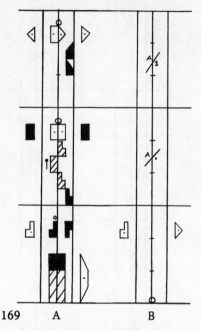

169   A   B

Fig. 169 shows two dancers, A and B. In the first bar, A moves; B merely raises her arms. In the second bar, B joins in doing the same pattern as A. In the third bar, B dances what A did in the first bar, while A has a new pattern.

Repeat Signs in the Column. When a small movement is repeated several times, it is easier to state the movement once and then to indicate with tiny repeat signs the number of times it is performed rather than write it out fully.

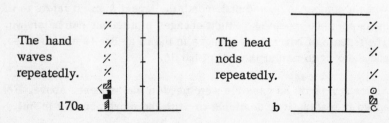

The hand waves repeatedly.   The head nods repeatedly.

170a   b

REPEAT SIGNS PLACED OUTSIDE THE STAFF

Shorter Sectional Repeats. When writing exercises or short
studies which are designed to be repeated several times, there is no
need to draft out each repeat as in a regular dance score. The exercise is written once and the repeats are indicated outside the staff.
The diagonal signs ⫫ and ⫰ are modified to ÷ and ≑ , and
are placed at the beginning and end of the section to be repeated.
Double bar lines enclose the section. To show a certain number of
repeats, a numeral is placed above the first repeat sign and below
the second. This describes the total number of times that the
sequence is performed.

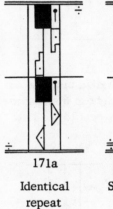
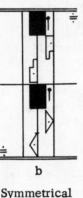
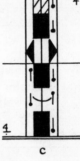

171a	b	c	d
Identical repeat	Symmetrical repeat	Total of 4 times, the same side.	Total of 8 times, alternating sides.

Longer Sectional Repeats. In
the case of longer sections in
which there may already be
smaller repeats, the double
lines at the beginning and end
of the section are extended out
on either side and the repeat
signs are drawn as extensions
of these lines. In this way
the repeat signs and the area
enclosed are easily visible.

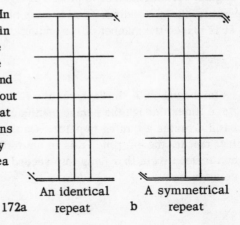

An identical repeat   172a   b   A symmetrical repeat

REPEATS USED WITH WAY SIGNS

The examples below show the placement of the way sign outside the repeat sign when it is not affected by the repeat, inside when it is affected.

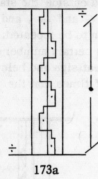

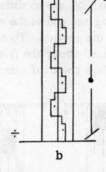

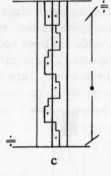

173a   b   c

| Take 12 steps to walk a complete circle. | Take 6 steps to walk a circle; two circles are walked in all. | Walk a circle to the right in 6 steps; repeat to the left. |

FIRST AND SECOND ENDING

The same device is used in Labanotation as in music notation to mark a change in the ending when a piece is repeated. An angular vertical bracket is placed alongside each of the two endings. Inside each bracket is placed the number of the ending.

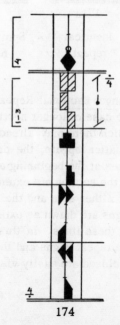

In the example shown here, the first three times through the phrase ending on bar 4 contains a turning in place. On the last repeat, the 4th time, this is omitted and instead there is a jump into second position.

174

LABELING OF SECTIONS - REPRISE SIGNS

When desired, a section can be labeled for
future reference. The section to be identified is
enclosed in double lines to which are attached
a box containing a letter or numeral. Later
on, when this section is repeated, the two reprise signs are written exactly the same way
at either end of an empty section of staff.

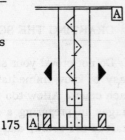

175

ENLARGEMENT OF SCORE

In writing a score, the length of the basic unit established is usually
kept constant. Do not make frequent changes if you can avoid them.
Any deviations from the basic unit must be indicated. Fast movements in which there is an extensive use of space require writing
many symbols and so for pieces in which this type of movement is
prevalent, the basic unit should be proportionately longer. However,
when an isolated case of quick, detailed movement appears in a
score that is otherwise slow and simple, it is best to write a general
indication of the movement in the score itself and place an enlarged
detailed description outside.

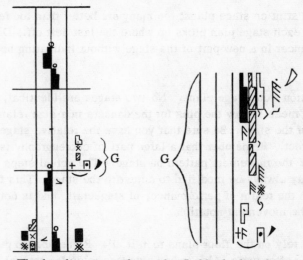

176

The bandit creeps forward. Suddenly he whips
out his gun and shoots. (The action is stylized.)

CLARIFICATIONS

DRAFTING THE SCORE

Do not crowd your score in order to save paper. It is not always easy to know immediately just how long a basic unit to take for each count. Allow too much space rather than too little. The three stages in preparing a score are: the rough notes, the first rough draft of the score, and the final neat copy in which all adjustments have been made.

Once you have established an order in the assignment of the staves, do not switch them around, for the reader quickly becomes accustomed to finding G or H in a certain place.

FLOOR PLANS

For complete stage plans, each diagram should give the identification of the dancers. In large group works, this may seem laborious, but it may be necessary to begin the study of a score in the middle, and the reader must be able to orientate himself quickly.

Do not stint on stage plans; too many are better than too few. Be sure that each stage plan picks up where the last left off. Do not show a dancer in a new part of the stage without indicating how he got there.

Proportion your stage plans. No two stages are identical, yet there is a mean. Draw the pins for the dancers in a size related to the size of the stage. Be sure that you have the relative stage positions correct. Remember that a large part of choreography is the spacing of the movement pattern on stage. The actual steps performed may always be modified to adjust to the stage. This factor belongs in the realm of performance, of stagecraft, and is not indicated in the movement notation.

Do not rely on the floor plans to tell all. Remember to put in facing pins after turns. Also, when a dancer holds for several measures, reiterate the stage pin when you come to a new page.

CHAPTER VIII

Touch, Slide, Brush

TOUCH

Touch, or contact, is one of the basic categories of movement. The notation is very simple: a horizontal, connecting bow.

177a

The connecting bow can be swung upward or downward, whichever interferes least with other writing on that part of the page.

By using the extremities of these bows, we have small upward or downward hooks.   177b

These small hooks are used to indicate contacting the floor while gesturing with the leg. The hook extends from the inside of the leg gesture symbol into the support column. In this respect, the support column represents the floor, and the hook shows the contact between the gesture and the floor.

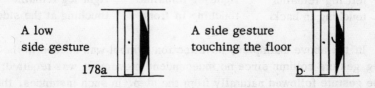

A low side gesture   A side gesture touching the floor

178a   b

Different types of hooks show the different parts of the foot which contact the floor: toe ⌎ ⌍ ; heel ⌐ ⌐ ; whole foot ≻ ≺.

Note the difference in the placement of the weight of the body in Fig. (a) where all the weight is on the left foot and the right is merely a touching gesture, and in Fig. (b) where the weight is equally divided on both feet.

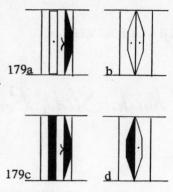

The same holds true in Figs. (c) and (d). In (c), there is no weight on the right leg, while in (d) there is some, though more weight is on the left leg since it is the lower support.

A clear distinction must be made between touching gestures and supports. Half supports - that is, gestures which take over some weight - do occur but are rare and will be dealt with in a later volume devoted to such subtle differences in movement.

TYPES OF TOUCH

Passive Touch. A passive touching gesture is one that occurs as the result of another movement. A typical example is seen at the end of a simple step. As the weight is transferred completely to one foot, the other is left touching the floor. Normally, the free leg is clear of the floor after a step, but in the cases cited below the contact with the floor is retained.

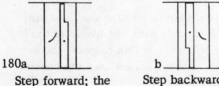

180a Step forward; the left leg remains touching in back.	b Step backward; the right leg remains touching in front.	c Step to the left; the right leg remains touching at the side.

In the above examples, no direction symbol was needed in the leg gesture column since no independent movement was required; the gesture followed naturally from the step. In such instances, the hook is drawn as though attached to a leg gesture symbol, extending closer to the outer staff line for the sake of easy reading.

Additional details in the performance of passive touching gestures can be shown by use of the flexing and extending symbols followed by a duration line.

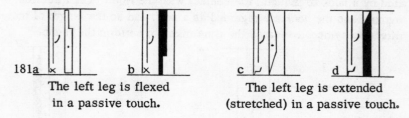

The left leg is flexed
in a passive touch.

The left leg is extended
(stretched) in a passive touch.

Occasionally it is important in a sequence that the foot does not shift or lift between a touch and a step. To indicate a step on the same spot in which a touch has just occurred, the staple is used. (See Chapter IV.)

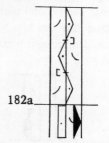

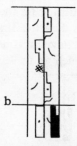

The swaying steps occur
always on the same spot.

There is an automatic moving
away from the previous spot
because of the length of step.

Active Touch. In contrast to the above, an active touch is a movement performed as a separate and distinct motion and, therefore, requiring the use of a direction symbol.

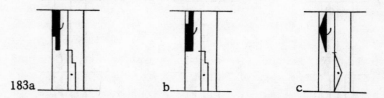

In each of the above instances, the leg is released from the floor before the touch occurs.

TIMING OF TOUCHING GESTURES

In touching gestures, the normally free gesture has been modified by a hook to indicate the contact with the floor. The direction symbol and the hook are regarded as a unit, and so the length of the direction symbol indicates the time taken to perform the touch.

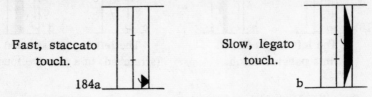

Fast, staccato touch.

Slow, legato touch.

184a   b

Fluent Transitions in Touches. A fluent touch occurs when there is a smooth transition from one part of the foot to another; for example, from the toe to the heel or vice versa. In such an action, the foot does not leave the floor. The direction symbol for the gesture shows the timing for the first part of the action; the second part is shown by a duration line. Without the duration line the touching hook would have no time indication and so would represent a quick, staccato touch as in Fig. 185 (c).

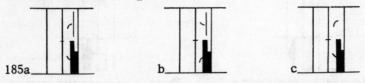

185a   b   c

Consecutive Touches. When active touching gestures appear one after the other, it is understood that the leg releases between each in order to be able to touch again. For repeated touches in the same direction it is not necessary to repeat the direction symbol, only the hooks need be drawn. However, if the rhythm should pose any problem, then direction symbols can be used for clarification.

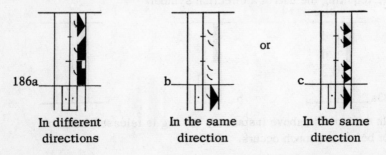

186a   b   or   c

In different directions | In the same direction | In the same direction

VARIATIONS IN TOUCHES

Distance of Touches. In a touching gesture, the foot contacts the floor at a comfortable distance from the support. To some degree the level of the support will determine the distance of the touch. When the support is in low level, the distance is greater. If the support is in high level, the touch must occur closer to the body.

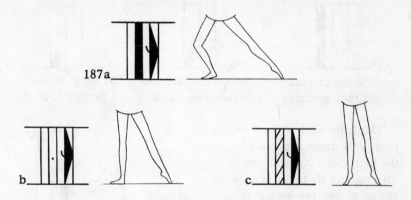

Often a touching gesture is bent. In these cases, the distance of the touch from the supporting foot may vary. The symbol × is used in the leg gesture column to indicate flexing. The distance of the touch from the center of weight is shown by placing the symbols × or ⌐ in the support column as indicated below. The idea is the same as for length of step. Fig. (a) illustrates a normal, comfortable distance of touch.

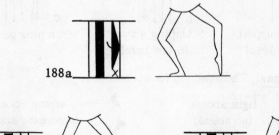

Releasing a Touch. The act of releasing between touching gestures can be performed for its own sake or for rhythmic purposes, in which case a release sign should be used. The action is a small movement spatially. The leg does not lift as high as a normal low gesture. The sign for release is ∿. This can also be written vertically ♩ when space demands. Note the difference in the movements described below.

189a

The leg touches
and then gestures.

b

The leg touches and
releases immediately.

c

The leg releases on
a particular beat.

Using the Ball of the Foot. In many folk dances it is the ball of the foot which contacts the floor. The sign for this part is a combination of the toe hook plus a straight line. Fig. (b) shows a typical step using this movement.

190a

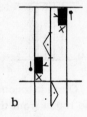

b

Stamps. A stamp is a support or a gesture in which the staccato contact with the ground produces a sound.

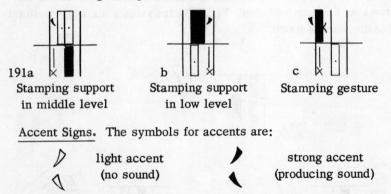

191a

Stamping support
in middle level

b

Stamping support
in low level

c

Stamping gesture

Accent Signs. The symbols for accents are:

$\mathcal{D}$ light accent
(no sound)

$\blacktriangleright$ strong accent
(producing sound)

As indicated in the examples above, a strong accent is used for a stamp. The small, wedge-shaped sign is placed next to the movement which it describes, with the point placed toward the symbol.

SLIDING

SLIDING LEG GESTURES

Continuous contact with the floor while performing a gesture results in a sliding gesture. This is indicated by using two of the same hooks - a progression on the same part of the foot.

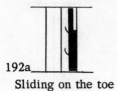 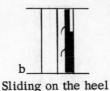 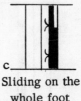

192a Sliding on the toe   b Sliding on the heel   c Sliding on the whole foot

The action of sliding can pass fluently from one part of the foot to another. In this case, different hooks are written on the one direction symbol.

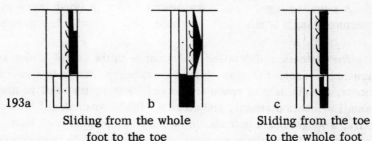

193a   b Sliding from the whole foot to the toe   c Sliding from the toe to the whole foot

The length of the symbol describes the duration of the sliding gesture. If nothing follows, the gesture remains touching the floor.

  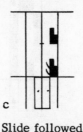 

194a Slide and hold (ends touching)   b Slide followed by a release   c Slide followed by a gesture   d Legato slide and gesture

BRUSHING

Sliding on the whole foot, especially when passing through place, is often called a brush. In performing a brush, a certain amount of pressure against the floor is understood. This is the natural result of the effort involved in keeping the whole foot in contact with the floor.

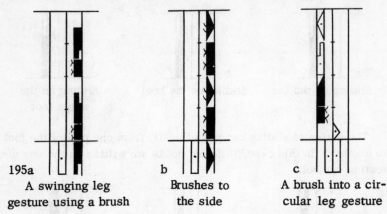

195a

A swinging leg
gesture using a brush

b

Brushes to
the side

c

A brush into a cir-
cular leg gesture

The indication of detailed performance in the use of slides and brushes is easiest in slow, legato movements. Where fast gestures occur, the problem of space arises and, with it, the need to draw small symbols distinctly and clearly. Where much detail is neces-sary, a longer basic unit should be used to represent each beat. Of course, the faster the movement, the less time there is to devote to exact performance of details.

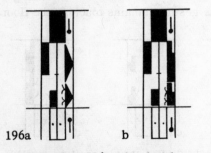

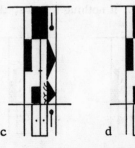

196a

b

c

d

An assemblé with a brush at
the beginning of the leg gesture

The same written with
more detail

Ballet Steps Using Brushes and Slides

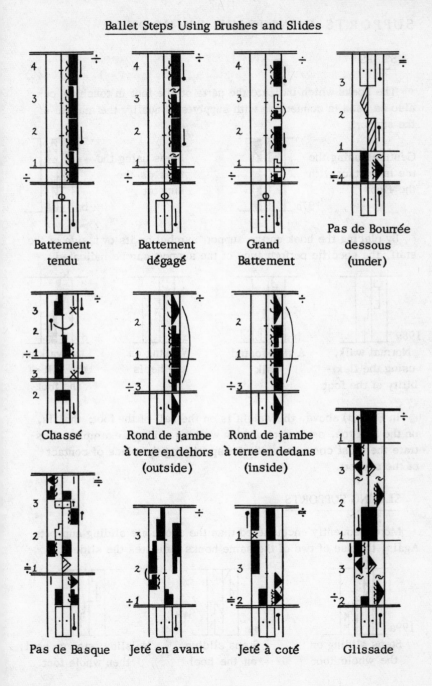

Battement
tendu

Battement
dégagé

Grand
Battement

Pas de Bourrée
dessous
(under)

Chassé

Rond de jambe
à terre en dehors
(outside)

Rond de jambe
à terre en dedans
(inside)

Pas de Basque   Jeté en avant   Jeté à coté   Glissade

SUPPORTS QUALIFIED BY HOOKS

STEPS

The hooks which indicate the parts of the foot in touching can also be used in connection with supports to qualify the manner of the support.

Gestures using the toe in contact with the floor

197a

Steps using the toes as the support

b

By placing the hook on the support symbol on its own side of the staff, the specific performance of the support can be indicated.

198a

b

c

d

Normal walk, using the flexibility of the foot.

A flat-footed walk

Walking on the heels

Low walk on the ball of the foot

In Fig. (d) above, the weight is on the ball of the foot; that is, on the half toe, as in normal high walking. These examples illustrate the most common needs for specifying the place of contact of the support.

SLIDING SUPPORTS

More frequently encountered than the above are sliding supports. Again, the use of two of the same hooks indicates the slide.

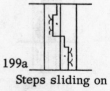

199a

b

c

Steps sliding on the whole foot

Steps sliding on the heel

No slide; step on heel, then whole foot.

In the preceding examples, the foot does not leave the floor in between each step. The sliding occurs as the weight is transferred. This is the motion used in skating. In skating, however, because of the pressure exerted and the smoothness of the ice, you continue to travel in space once the sliding step has been taken. This traveling is shown by means of way signs. Note Fig. 199 (c) where the use of two different hooks indicates a stylized walk and not a sliding step.

In writing slides, a clear distinction must be made between a gesture and a support. Note the difference between Figs. (a) and (b). Where a gesture is used, the weight of the body remains in place. In a step, the weight begins to travel at once into the direction stated.

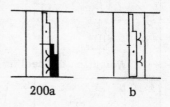

200a   b

VARIATIONS OF THE BASIC SUPPORTS

For general use, the simple levels of support - middle, high, and low - suffice. However, variations of these often appear, primarily in national dances. These variations are caused by different uses of the foot and by flexing the knees. To show finer degrees, we use an enlarged scale of hooks to represent the parts of the foot.

Key to Parts of the Foot. Note the different uses of the ball of the foot. In addition to the normal 1/2 toe there is the higher 3/4 toe (high arch) and a lower use with the heel closer to the floor. The small circles indicating these differences - white for up and black for down - are derived from the relationship pins.

These hooks are used in connection with the floor. To show a hand touching a certain part of the foot, the body area or limb sign for that part must be used. These are given in a later chapter.

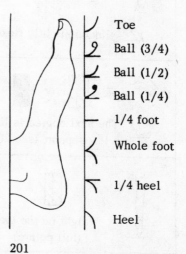

Toe

Ball (3/4)

Ball (1/2)

Ball (1/4)

1/4 foot

Whole foot

1/4 heel

Heel

201

Variations of Middle Level.

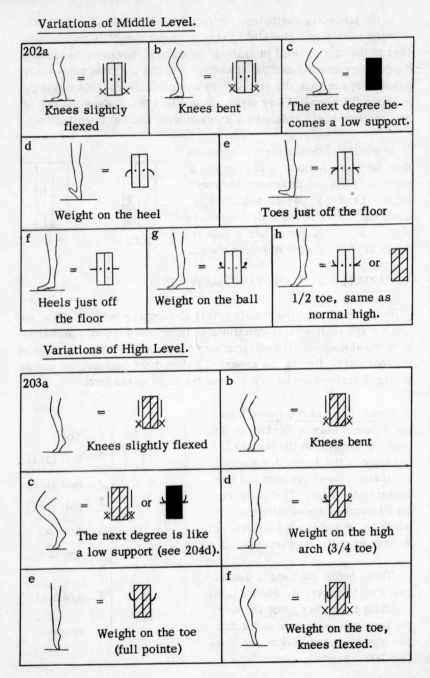

202a Knees slightly flexed

b Knees bent

c The next degree becomes a low support.

d Weight on the heel

e Toes just off the floor

f Heels just off the floor

g Weight on the ball

h 1/2 toe, same as normal high.

Variations of High Level.

203a Knees slightly flexed

b Knees bent

c The next degree is like a low support (see 204d).

d Weight on the high arch (3/4 toe)

e Weight on the toe (full pointe)

f Weight on the toe, knees flexed.

Variations of Low Level.

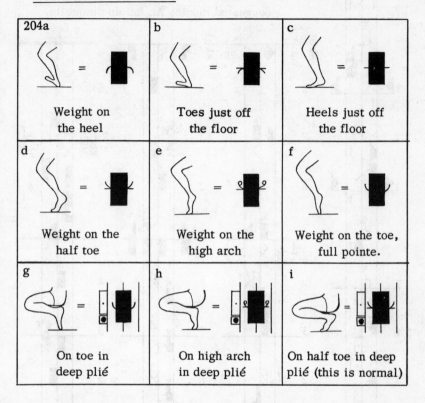

In describing a support, it is important to determine into which basic category a support belongs - middle, high, or low - and then to add the necessary modifications. As can be seen, the results are often rather similar in appearance, and it may be the feeling of the step that will determine whether it is in the high level with flexed knees, for example, or the low with raised heels category. In a deep knee bend, even though the heels are raised, the support cannot be called high. As far as the body is concerned, it is a low support and so must be written that way with the necessary details, such as weight on the ball of the foot, added. It is rare for a deep knee bend (plié) to be performed with the heels remaining on the floor; that is, the whole foot contacting. However, it can be done and sometimes appears in choreography. To indicate this, you merely add the hooks for the whole foot to the low support sign.

STUDY IN TOUCH AND SLIDE
Suggested music: An Italian tarantella.

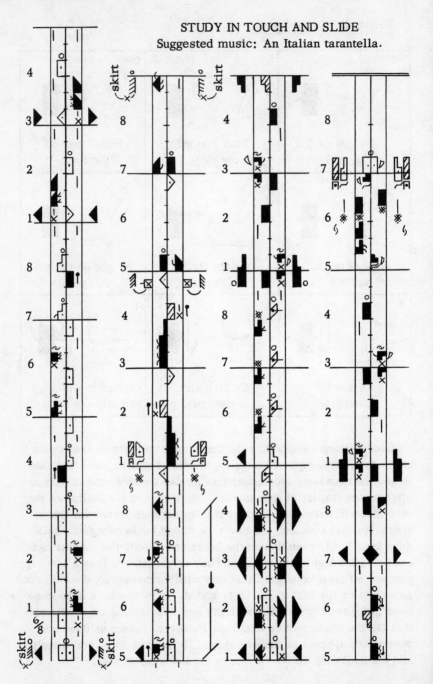

CLARIFICATIONS

The whole subject of touching and brushing the floor is usually understood rather easily. In writing, however, special care should be taken in placing the hooks on the direction symbols. The idea behind the hooks is to show the connection (the contact) between the leg gesture and the support column (representing the floor). Therefore, the hooks attached to leg gestures extend toward the support column. In the case of sliding supports, the reverse is true. The hooks on the support symbols extend into the leg gesture column to show how the support is performed.

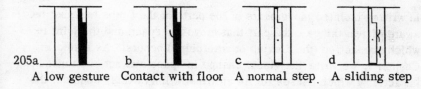

205a   A low gesture   b Contact with floor   c A normal step   d A sliding step

Note the placement of the hooks in the examples below.

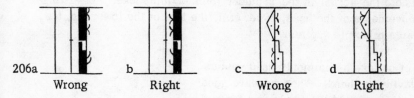

206a   Wrong   b Right   c Wrong   d Right

The use of hooks to indicate touches and slides is a good example of how major movement patterns may be modified in notation. Any step which employs a slide can also be done without one. This would be the basic, simple form. By indicating the slide, the whole style of performance is changed, although the basic structure remains intact.

CHAPTER IX

The Parts of the Limbs

In writing isolated movements of the parts of the limbs we must be aware of two things - the part that moves in space and the joint in which the action (the flexing or stretching) occurs. As stated in Chapter I, we write the visual change in space and not the muscular activity which causes it. As an illustration of this, consider the gestures of the arms and legs. To record these we write the direction in space into which the whole arm or leg moves; we do not record the action in the shoulder joint or hip socket. In writing movements of the hand, lower arm, the foot or the lower leg, the same principle applies.

Let us take a commonly used gesture - waving the hand. When we wave good-bye, we extend the whole arm forward high and follow it with a repeated motion of the hand. The hand lifts and lowers; it moves in space, but the action takes place in the wrist. The hand motion is actually the result of the flexing and ex-  207 tending of the wrist. However, we usually describe the action as one of the hand going up and down and so the appropriate direction symbols will follow the special sign for the hand. If we were told to flex and extend the wrist, a rather similar action would occur, but with a different emphasis and expression. This would be written with the special sign for the wrist followed by the symbols X and ⌐ . Where it provides a better movement description, this action in the joint is written. However, this description is less commonly used and so we will deal first with the path in space of the limb.

THE SPECIFIC PARTS OF THE BODY

This illustration shows all the joint signs which will be used and discussed in this chapter. These are pre-signs and are placed in front of the direction symbol.

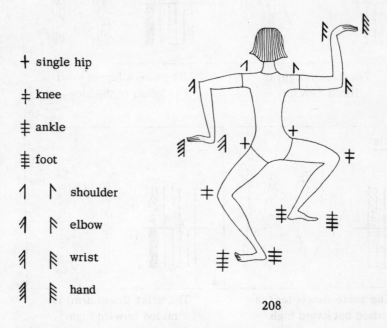

+ single hip

‡ knee

‡ ankle

‡ foot

↑ ↾ shoulder

↿ ↾ elbow

↿ ↾ wrist

↿ ↾ hand

208

You will notice that the shoulder and arm joints are written differently for the right side and the left. In contrast, there is only one set of signs for the parts of the leg. Right and left for these are shown by where the symbols are placed on the staff; that is, right or left of the center line.

The best image to bear in mind in learning the notation of the parts of the limbs is that of a puppet, the kind with strings attached to each joint. Puppets follow the instructions (the strings that are pulled) perfectly, since they are relaxed and allow for the natural pull of gravity. Although we do not move as limply as puppets, but introduce dynamics and flow of movement into our actions, our use of space - that is, of direction and level - is identical with theirs.

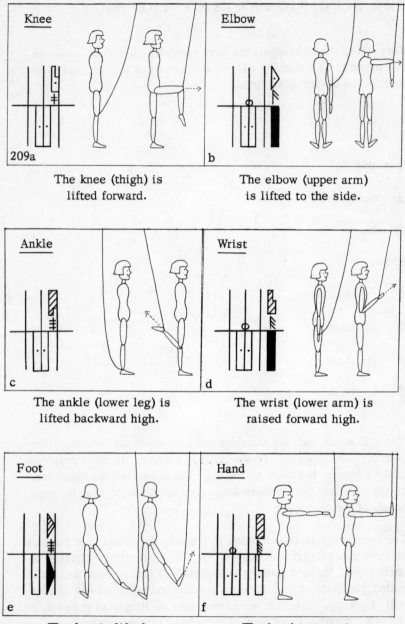

The knee (thigh) is
lifted forward.

The elbow (upper arm)
is lifted to the side.

The ankle (lower leg) is
lifted backward high.

The wrist (lower arm) is
raised forward high.

The foot is lifted
side high.

The hand is raised
place high.

PARTS OF THE LEG

THE HIP

In writing movements of the hips we must be clear as to whether one hip is leading or being emphasized; whether both hips are involved; or whether the whole area, the pelvic girdle, is being used as a unit. Of course, because of the structure of the human body, one hip cannot be moved without the other's being affected. Usually the passive hip moves in the opposite direction to the active, or leading, hip. The normal position for the hip is place middle, since it can be raised or lowered in place.

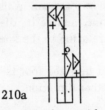

210a

Swaying from side to side with parallel hip action

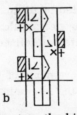

b

Hula step; the hip is lifted on the leg that remains touching.

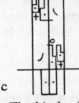

c

The hip leads forward with each step.

THE UPPER LEG (THIGH)

The knee guides the movements of the thigh. We are accustomed to lifting the knee while marching or skipping, so that we are aware of this use. Direction and level for the knee are the same as for the whole leg. When picking up the knee, the lower leg just follows passively, hanging straight down.

211

Drum Majorette

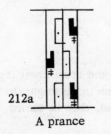

212a

A prance

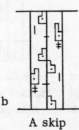

b

A skip

c

High knee extension

THE LOWER LEG

The ankle guides the movements in space of the lower leg.
The isolated use of this part is
not so common, but it appears in
many dance forms, the most popular of which is doubtless the can-
can. In this step, the upper leg is
held out while the lower leg beats
rapidly in and out or describes cir-

213

Can-can

cles. Physiologically, the lower leg is limited in its range. However, its movements in space can be varied according to the placement of the upper leg and also by means of passive rotations in the
hip joint. The lower leg moves from the knee joint, and so its direction and level in space are determined by its relation to the knee.

In the performance of movements of the lower leg, the foot is
carried along passively. If the foot points in another direction, it
must be written separately.

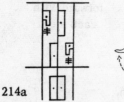 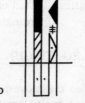

214a

b

The lower leg is raised straight
back on each change.

The thigh remains out to the
side, only the lower leg moves.

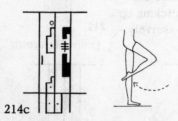 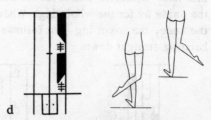

214c

d

The thigh remains in the
forward low direction, only
the lower leg moves back.

Here the movement of the lower leg
causes a rotation in the thigh: first
it is out-turned, then in-turned.

THE FOOT

The foot symbol is used to describe movements of the foot in space.   To get the right idea, you must think of the tip of the foot guiding the action. As with the lower leg, the foot is limited in its range of movement, its use of direction and level being determined by what has happened or is happening to the rest of the leg. The foot moves from the ankle joint and so takes its direction and level from there.

As with the lower leg, movements of the foot can cause a passive rotation in the hip joint. The leg and the foot are kept in line; that is, there is a straight line from the center of the knee through the center of the foot. Twisting or curling movements of the foot, such as are used in therapeutic exercises, are rotations of the foot and ankle. These are discussed in a later chapter.

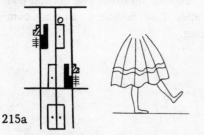

215a

Peasant Dance: The foot is turned up on each gesture. Note that the foot can be written in the third column when the column is not otherwise being used.

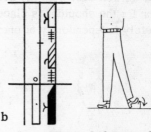

b

Impatience: Lifting and tapping the foot.

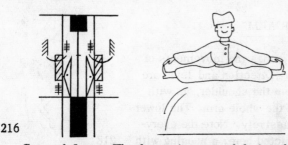

216

Cossack Jump: The feet point upward during the jump.
Note the indication of contact between the foot and the hand.

PARTS OF THE ARM

Movements of the parts of the arm are very similar to those of the leg. The chief difference lies in the greater range resulting from the greater flexibility in the arm joints.

THE SHOULDER

The shoulders have limited but very distinct movements. The most commonly used are the lifting of the shoulders in shrugging and the pulling back of the shoulders in order to achieve good army posture. In any shoulder movement, the action is in the shoulder blade, and the range will depend on the individual build. Some people are much more flexible in this area than others, and cases have been known of complete flexibility where no collar bone existed. But we will deal with the average range of motion. The normal position for the shoulder is place middle. The shoulders can work completely independently of one another.

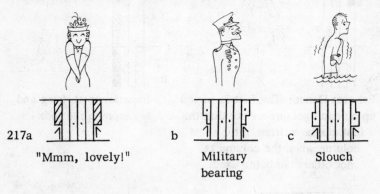

217a

"Mmm, lovely!"

b

Military
bearing

c

Slouch

THE UPPER ARM

The elbow guides the movements of the upper arm. Direction and level are determined from the shoulder, as with movements of the whole arm. The lower arm follows passively. Note the everyday action depicted here, a nudging with the elbow.

218

"Hey, look!"

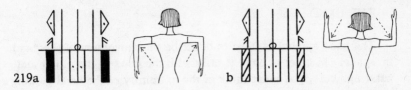

219a   b

Note the different results in the two examples above. The final position of the upper arm (the elbow) is the same in both cases, but the different starting positions produce a different result in the lower arm. In each case the lower arm has followed the upper arm in space without changing its original direction.

THE LOWER ARM

The wrist guides the movements of the lower arm. The hand does not follow limply, but is used as a passive extension of the lower arm. Due to the structure of the elbow, the lower arm is limited in its range of action. Its movements in space will depend on the placement of the upper arm. Direction and level for the lower arm are determined by its relation to the elbow from which it moves. Movements of the lower arm may cause passive rotations in the shoulder joint. These rotations are unimportant since they occur only to accommodate the actions of that part of the arm.

An everyday example of a movement of the lower arm is the military salute. While the performer is aware of the hand approaching the forehead, the motion is not one of the hand, but rather one of the arm from the elbow down.

220   Military salute

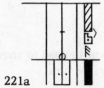

221a   b

The lower arm is lifted until it is straight above the elbow from which it moves. It has performed a half circle.

Starting with the whole arm to the side, the lower arm moves up and to the other side, ending with the hand over the shoulder.

THE HAND

The hand symbol is used to describe the movement of the hand in space. In order to have it tally with the uses of the elbow and wrist symbols, you must think of the extremity of the hand guiding the movement. The exact direction and level in space used will depend on the placement of the arm. It is important, therefore, to write these first. The hand moves from the wrist, so its direction and level will be determined by its relation to the wrist.

Simple movements of the hand follow the same general pattern as those of the foot but, with its tremendous flexibility, the hand can perform so many more movements that it must be given a great deal of individual attention and analysis. For many gestures of the hand it is important to state where the palm faces. When the hand takes a new direction, the palm faces the direction which requires the least effort - that is, the most natural one. For details on facing of the palms, see Chapter XI.

222a   "Stop!"   b   Egyptian style

USE OF BOWS WITH PARTS OF THE BODY

BOW FOR SIMULTANEOUS MOVEMENT

As discussed in Chapter V, a small curved bow is used to show that two movements are to be performed at the same time.

First the knee is
raised and then
the lower leg
is drawn in.   223a

Both these actions
occur at once, as
indicated by
the bow.   b

First the whole
leg is raised,
then the foot
moves upward. 224a

Both these ac-
tions occur
at once.   b

The correct way for writing all parts of the limb movements is to start with the center, the part closest to the body and work out.

Simultaneous movement can also be shown by placing the symbols side by side. For leg gestures, this means encroaching into the third column which is used for the body. As long as the body column is free and the pre-sign for the part of the leg is used, this is permissible. When fast movements are being written, there is often not enough space for them in the leg gesture column, so the side-by-side method may be used.

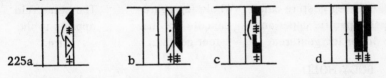

225a   b   c   d

BOW FOR THE SAME PART OF THE BODY

It is not necessary to repeat the same pre-sign each time when movements of the same part of the body are being described. The repeated pre-sign is both time and space consuming. Movements of the same part are connected by an angular bow: ⟩ . These bows are used in all cases in which the parts and the whole of a limb are written in the same column.

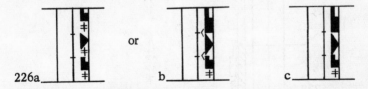

226a   or   b   c

In Figs. (a) and (b) each gesture is one of the knee. In Fig. (c) the absence of this bow means that only the first movement is done by the knee; the subsequent ones are gestures of the whole leg. A direction symbol in the leg column without a pre-sign or without an angular bow indicates a movement of the whole leg. The bow can be placed on either side of the symbol.

USE OF HOLD SIGNS FOR THE LIMBS

CANCELLATIONS

Since the movements of the whole limb affect the various parts which it comprises, any gesture of an individual part will be cancelled by a subsequent movement of the whole. In order to retain a particular position, for instance of the hand or foot, a hold sign must be used.

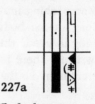

227a · Whole leg gesture cancels specific upper and lower leg gestures.

b · Whole leg gesture cancels specific foot gesture.

c · The same rule applies to the arm.

BODY HOLD

The use of the hold sign O for parts of the body was introduced in Chapter VI. When used as a body hold, it means that that part of the body retains its relation (or position) to the body.

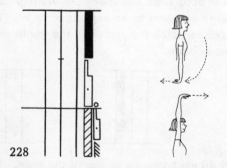

228

In this figure the arm starts straight up, with the hand gesturing forward. The hand is given a hold sign, and so it retains this position (that is, the flexed wrist) while the arm moves forward and down. This hold sign for a part of the body remains until either a new direction is written for that part or a back to normal sign is used.

SPACE HOLD

The space hold sign was introduced in Chapter VI. There we were concerned with its use in connection with turning. It can also be used to show that one part of a limb retains its space relation in spite of an action by another part.

Here the arm starts straight up with the hand gesturing forward. But as the arm is lowered through forward to place low, the hand maintains its space relation; i.e., its horizontal-forward direction from the wrist.

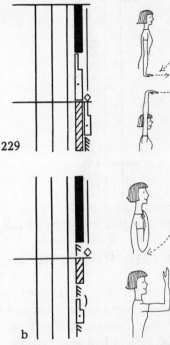

229

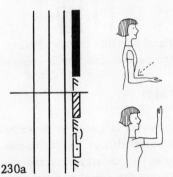

230a

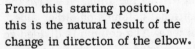

From this starting position, this is the natural result of the change in direction of the elbow.

b

Because the lower arm has been given a space hold, it remains vertically above the elbow.

When a movement as described above occurs in conjunction with a turn, it may be desirable for clarification to state the direction into which the limb has moved at the end of the space hold action. This direction symbol is tied to the duration line following the space hold to indicate the unity in movement.

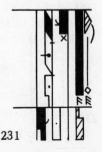

231

BACK TO NORMAL

The symbol for back to normal is ☉ . The meaning is to return to the normal state, or normal body position. It is used to cancel any special use of the body, such as twisting, flexing, or a particular use of space. It may also be used to cancel the hold sign.

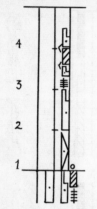

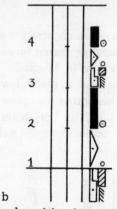

232a
Foot position holds until a new direction is written for it.

b
Hand position is cancelled on the second and fourth counts.

DIVISION OF THE COLUMN

The leg and the arm columns can be divided in order to describe the movements of the upper and lower parts without having to use the space-consuming pre-signs. This is particularly advantageous in the case of fast leg gestures. In writing the arms, you have the advantage of being able to use additional columns on either side. This is not always possible for the legs. The column is divided so that very slender direction symbols are used. Note that the upper part of the limb is written closest to the center. Through this device, the third column need not be used.

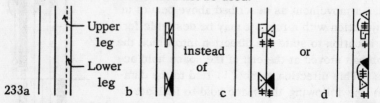

233a b instead of c or d

Examples of the passé and attitude leg gestures used in ballet.

STUDY IN BALLET STYLE
(Use of Parts of the Leg)

Suggested music: The Coda of Act II
from the "Swan Lake" ballet.

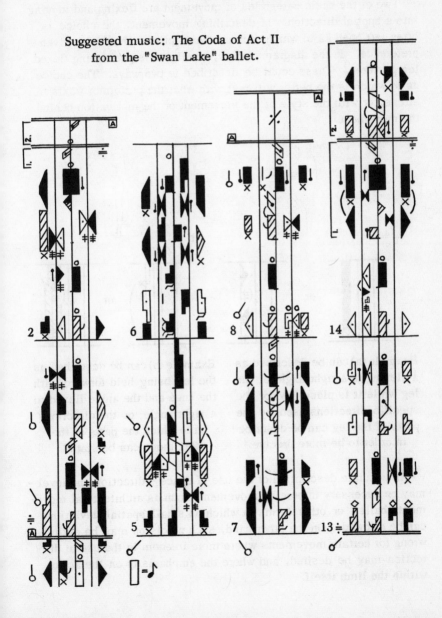

CLARIFICATIONS

CHOICE OF DESCRIPTION

Two of the basic categories of movement are flexing and moving into a spatial direction. In describing movement, the choice is often left open as to which of these descriptions should be given preference. In the diagrams below, the figure is performing flexed leg gestures. These could be described in two ways. The choice as to which is the better will rest with what the performer wants to stress, or with the style of the movement or the motivation behind the movement.

234a   b

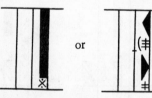   or   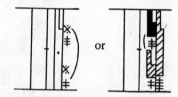   or

Example (a) can be described as a flexing to a right angle of the leg while it is place low; or the specific directions used by the parts of the leg can be described in order to be more precise.

Example (b) can be described as the leg being held forward with the knee and the ankle flexed to a right angle; or the directions into which the parts of the leg move can be stated.

An accurate description of the use of space - direction and level - may be necessary in precise movement, such as architectural movement, ballet, or other forms in which no small spatial deviations can be allowed. On the other hand, such precision may be entirely wrong for certain movements where more freedom in the use of direction may be desired, and where the emphasis is on the action within the limb itself.

CHAPTER X

Passive Movements, Uses of the Body

PASSIVE MOVEMENTS

Many movement patterns comprise elements that are active (leading) and passive (following). In others, one part of the body moves in unison with or accompanies another. The movement of a part of a limb, therefore, may be described in any one of three ways as leading, accompanying, or following. These possible variations are illustrated below by the man and his dog.

235a Leading   b Accompanying   c Following

Now let us consider the analagous case of a limb. The hand (dog) may lead the arm (Fig. a); may move in unison with the arm (Fig. b); or may be led by it (Fig. c).

236a Leading   b Accompanying   c Following

In the case of the isolated movements of parts of the limbs, the movements of the upper limbs cause a passive path in space to be made by the lower limbs. Perhaps the best example of this is the path in space of the lower leg when led by the action of the knee.

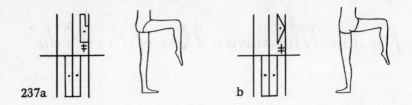

The knee leads or motivates the action. Because the lower leg reacts passively, it follows the law of gravity and so hangs straight down in space. This is understood; only the main action need be notated.

In some arm movements, however, the lower limb would normally be carried along with the arm, as an extension of it (accompanying movement). Then, if a passive movement is desired, it must be indicated separately. In the examples below, one is written simply; the other includes a passive reaction in a part of the arm. The sign for passive is a broken, dotted line, placed in the appropriate column. A specific part of the body may also be shown to be passive, as indicated below.

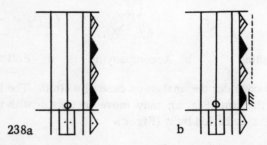

Fig. (a) shows a waving movement of the whole arm. Fig. (b) shows the same thing, but the hand is indicated as being passive, hence it will follow the arm movement, much like a scarf being waved in the breeze. The part that is passive must be relaxed so that it may be influenced by the active part. It has no will of its own but is led into the path it takes.

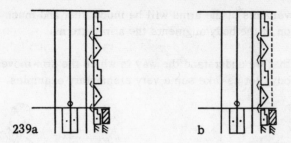

Fig. (a) shows a starting position with the elbow forward and the lower arm straight up. As the elbow is moved to the side and forward again, the lower arm moves with it but remains vertical in space. In Fig. (b) the lower arm is shown to be passive; it will therefore follow the leading movement of the upper arm and will not remain strictly vertical.

Passive movements are purposely not too exactly defined. The range of the movement will depend a great deal on its speed and latitude. Degrees can be shown within the passive sign, the symbols × and ⌐ referring to the lesser or greater use of space and not to the flexing or extending of the limb itself.

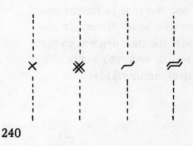

240

ARM-AND-BODY MOVEMENTS

A direction symbol in the arm column indicates a gesture of the arm alone. The body should not join in these movements at all, except for the few instances where there must be flexibility in the shoulder area to facilitate performance.

However, in this chapter we are giving the body more freedom in allowing it to take part in the movements of the arms. The important thing to remember is that the body is not doing a movement on its own; it is merely being carried along by the action of the arm. What occurs in the body would not occur at all but for the motivation of the arm. If the body is not held still, the swinging and circular movements of the arms will be much freer and much larger. The inclusion of the body augments the arm patterns.

To be sure that we understand the way in which the arm movements affect the body, let us take some very elementary examples.

241

If you reach for an object that is close at hand, you need merely extend the arm to pick it up. But if it is further away, you will have to include the body, the part nearest to that arm, in order to reach the object comfortably.

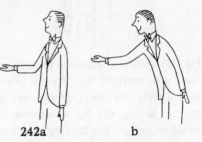

242a   b

Here is a person shaking hands. Because no body movement is used, he seems cold, stand-offish. If you like a person, you incline toward him, and so Fig. (b) shows a person who is not holding back; an out-going warm-hearted type.

243a   b

Fig. (a) shows a student surreptitiously passing a note in class. The movement is one of the arm alone. Fig. (b) shows how she does it when she has permission. Where freedom of motion is allowed, she will automatically include the body.

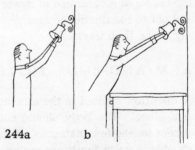

244a   b

Fig. (a) is a person using both hands to fix a light bulb which is forward high but within easy reach. In Fig. (b) the person is unable to get near the light, and so must include the upper body in the action.

Many of these everyday uses of arm-and-body movements occur in dance. The chief difference is that they are done for their own sake and not for a functional purpose. In daily life, we use our arms as much as possible in front of the body. In dance, use is made of all directions.

One of the most difficult arm-alone movements is crossing the arm into the opposite side-high direction, as shown in Fig. (a). By including the body, the movement is made easier to perform and more attractive to look at.

245a   b

THE INCLUSION BOWS

To show that a part of the body is included in another movement, a vertical bow is used. There are two of these bows, one to show only a slight inclusion and the other to show a definite inclusion. At this point we are not interested in very exact performance, but rather in the general description. Note that the part included is always the one nearest the moving limb; for example, the shoulder area when the arm moves.

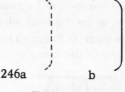

246a   b

Slight   Definite
inclusion   inclusion

247a

Arm alone

b

A slight inclusion

c

A definite inclusion

d

Arm alone

e

A slight inclusion

f

A definite inclusion

The inclusion bow is drawn from the arm symbol into the body column (the third column on either side). It has a time value: the inclusion starts where the bow starts. It is also a "passing state" in that, once the inclusion bow ceases and another arm movement occurs, the previous inclination of the body is automatically cancelled.

248a   b

In Fig. (a) both arms are swinging, but it is only the right arm that includes the body. This will produce a one-sided effect, with the body inclining and also twisting slightly forward and then backward. In Fig. (b) both arms include the body. This means equal influence; hence the body will remain upright but will rotate (twist) from side to side, first left and then right.

It is important to be aware of the different effects that arm movements have on the body when only one arm is used; when both arms exert an equal influence; and when the direction of the movement is lateral, or in the forward-backward area.

249a

The upper body tilts to the side only. (See Fig. 241.)

b

The upper body tilts forward and twists slightly to the left.
(See Fig. 242b)

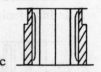

c

Only a tilt forward occurs. The double-sided action negates any twist. (See Fig. 244.)

d

Only a twist occurs. The double-sided action negates any tilt.

SPECIFIC MOVEMENTS OF THE BODY

To describe the movements of the body more specifically, we analyze the torso into its individual parts.

◰	◼	◱	☒	C	ᶜ
Chest	Pelvic	Whole	Waist	Head	Face
250	girdle	torso			

The chest is sometimes called the rib cage, or the center of lightness. The pelvic girdle is the hip area and is also considered the
center of weight. The whole torso, it will be noted, is a combination of the chest and pelvic girdle signs written as a unit. The
waist, though written as an area, does not move into space as a
limb but is rather the hinge for the movements of the chest and pelvic girdle. The waist is chiefly used for touching, as in putting the
hand on the waist, and for lifting, as in partner work. The head is
indicated by the letter C (capus). This symbol describes movements
in space in which the head is used much like a limb. By boxing the
C, we indicate an area sign; that is, the face. A direction sign
following the boxed C means turning to face, or to look into that
direction.

The different categories of movement that can be performed by
these parts are tilting, rotating, shifting, facing.

By tilting we mean inclining, bowing, or bending. This meaning of
the word bending should not be confused with flexing. Rotary movements are, of course, twists in the body. Shifting is the displacement in space of a body area away from its normal position, the
movement usually being on a horizontal plane. Facing means turning toward the direction stated and presenting the front of the body
area squarely to that direction.

Movements of the body frequently embrace combinations of these
basic categories. In this chapter we will deal with each one individ-
ually. We will not, however, touch on the matter of rotations since
it brings up certain problems which must be treated in detail. However, many rotary movements can be written in other ways. The
use of the body inclusion in gestures of the arms will take care of

some of these. Others can be described by facing of the head or
chest.   Through these and through the use of shifting and tilting,
many movements of the torso and its parts can now be written.

Below are charted the various movements of the body. Note that the
normal position for each is place high.

	Tilting	Rotating	Shifting	Facing
Head c				
Chest				
		Chest has its own column		
Whole torso				
Pelvic girdle				

251

TILTING

The Head. The head is normally held place high, straight above the neck. The head moves from the neck. A clear distinction must be made from the start between the use of the head as a limb and its use as a face which can look, see, and focus on outside objects or points in space. The symbol C represents the head used as a limb. In this capacity it performs such daily motions as saying yes (nodding), saying no, shaking from side to side, dropping as when falling asleep, or rolling in order to relax the neck muscles. In dance, similar motions are used for purposes of enhancing the design of the body line. In touching or supporting C represents the top of the head.

The head is written on the right side of the staff, in the sixth column out. This is not a fixed home for the head. It may be moved out or written close in if space demands. Since the pre-sign for the head is always used, there is no question about which part of the body is intended.

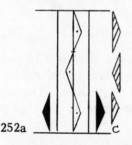

252a   b

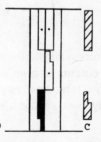

The head participates in tilts of the chest and whole torso, being carried along as an extension of the spine. However, the head may also make a definite gesture as in Fig. 253(a).

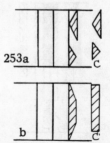

253a

If, during a tilt of the body, the head stays upright, this must be written.

b

By using the neck vertebrae alone, the head can tilt only in high level. For it to tilt to middle level, the dorsal vertebrae must be used; for tilting to low level, the body must be included.

The Whole Torso. The whole torso moves in one piece from the hips, and so its level and direction are determined from there. Normally it is held straight up from the hips.

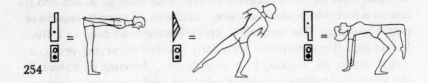

254

The whole torso can also be stretched (extended through the spine) or rounded (through the curving of the spine). For these, the symbols $\times$ and $\frown$ are used in the same way as for the arm.

255

Whole torso movements are written in the left third column. Since this column is also used for the pelvic girdle, the pre-sign for the whole torso is always used for clarification. The same part of the body bow should also be used when the pre-sign is not repeated.

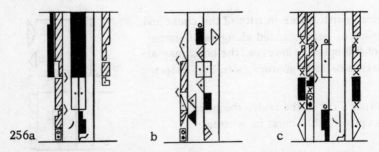

256a   b   c

Tilting movements of the whole torso are often comparatively small in space. For these, it is necessary to use in-between directions, which will be discussed in Chapter XI.

The Chest. The chest or rib cage is that area of the body, above the waist, which uses the waist as its axis of movement. Its normal position is straight up above the waist. From a standing position, the chest cannot tilt to horizontal level (waist level) without some giving way in the lower spine. Any displacement of the lower spine in conjunction with a movement of the chest usually falls under the heading of a whole torso movement.

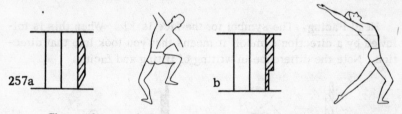

257a

Chest tilting side high

b

Chest tilting back high

Tilting of the chest is written in the right third column without any pre-sign. This column is reserved for the chest, and any direction symbol not preceded by some other pre-sign will mean tilting of the chest. The pre-sign for the chest is reserved to describe the facing of the chest into different directions. Because of the flexibility of the ribs, the chest can stretch and flex, ⌐ and × .

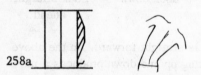

258a

Chest is stretched, extended.

b

Chest is flexed, rounded.

The chest can also move simultaneously with, but independently, of the whole torso. In the example here the whole torso is forward middle while the chest is place high.

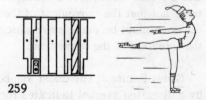

259

The chest also uses in-between directions; for instance, in ballet, where the movements of the upper torso are very subtle and often involve only slight deviations from the normal position.

FACING

The action of facing means turning to look into a direction. To face a person or a direction on stage means to turn so that the front of the body is toward that person or direction. Facing with the head means looking. Facing with the chest means presenting the front of the chest to that direction.

Head Facing. The symbol for the face is ⓒ . When this is followed by a direction symbol, it means that you look into that direction. Note the difference in writing of tilting and facing.

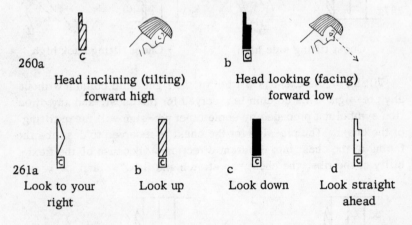

260a   Head inclining (tilting)
        forward high

b   Head looking (facing)
        forward low

261a   Look to your   b   Look up   c   Look down   d   Look straight
        right   ahead

The normal position for facing is straight forward. In the above examples, you will note that looking up and down produces a motion similar to that of tilting the head backward and forward. But the motivation is quite different. When looking or facing, the eyes and the face itself have a focus, and outside space becomes important, not just the movement of the body within itself. In writing, a decision must be made as to which way of writing best expresses the intention of the movement.

Chest Facing. The chest symbol followed by a direction symbol indicates the facing of the chest. The chest does not have the range and freedom of movement of the head, and so its facing movements are limited. Normally, 262 the chest faces forward middle.

SHIFTING

By shifting we mean moving in a straight path, like a box resting on a table being pushed a few inches one way or the other. Because it is a path, no matter how small, we relate the way of writing it to the writing of the straight way signs.

┬
┴ Sign for a
    straight path

Straight path
for the chest

Straight path
for the head

The body area sign is modified to indicate that a shift is to be described. The direction of the shift is shown by the direction symbols which follow the pre-sign.

The body areas which can shift are: the head, the chest, the pelvic girdle, and the whole torso. The whole torso, however, must be held in one piece in shifting, so its scope is small.

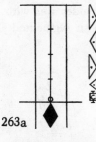

263a
A side-to-side shift. The well-known Hindu head motion.

b
A shift of the chest from side to side

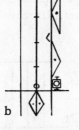

c
A swaying forward and back-ward of the whole torso

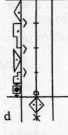

d
A circle of the pelvic girdle

Normal Position. The normal position for a shift is place middle. The return to normal can be written by using this direction or by using the back to normal sign ⊙ .

Degree of Shifting. A smaller or a larger path can be shown by means of the symbols × and ⌐ . These are placed in front of the direction symbol, their interpretation being the same as for length of step.   264

THE SHOULDER AREA

Movements in the upper spine are described by using the symbol
for the shoulder area:

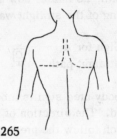

⊡ right shoulder area

⊡ left shoulder area

⊞ both shoulder areas

Movements in the shoulder area
do not affect the lower dorsal   265
spine. There should be no displacement of the chest.

The individual shoulder area can extend in space. It is often used
for movements of the upper body similar to those that occur when
an arm gesture extends far in space and pulls the shoulder area with
it (Fig. a). A shoulder area movement (Fig. b) is like an augmented
shoulder movement.

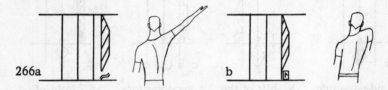

266a   b

When the double shoulder area sign is indicated, its use is similar to that of the chest, in that the shoulder area tilts and rotates.
The range of movement, however, is much more limited.

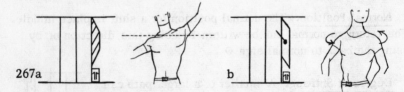

267a   b

It is these small movements of the shoulder area that are used
in the ballet épaulement.

STUDY IN BODY AND ARM MOVEMENTS

Suggested music: Brahms' "Lullaby."

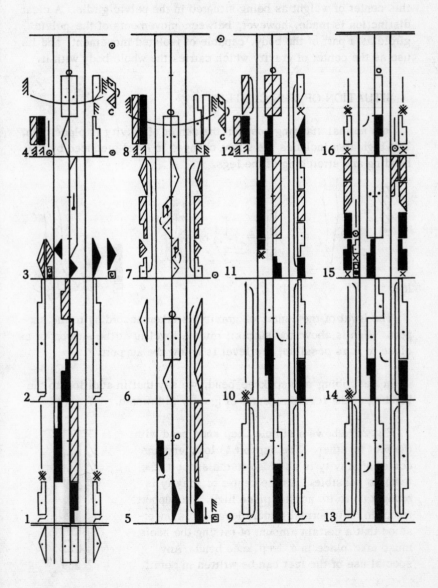

THE CENTER OF GRAVITY

The center of gravity represents the center of weight of the whole body. The placement of the weight is very important in correctly understanding and performing many types of movements. We regard this center of weight as being situated in the pelvic girdle. A clear distinction is made, however, between movements of the pelvic girdle as a part of the body, capable of isolated movement, and its use as the center of gravity which carries the whole body with it.

SITUATION OF THE CENTER

In a normal standing position the center of gravity is place high. The high area includes the slight changes in level produced by the bending and stretching of the legs.

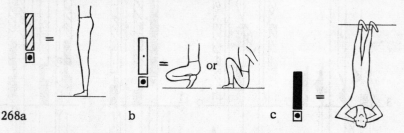

268a   b   c

The level of the center of gravity is taken according to the support. High is above the support; middle level is at the support or as close to it as possible; low level is below the support.

In describing a deep knee bend, we say that in addition to the bending of the legs the center of gravity is lowered.

Fig. 269 shows a simple deep knee bend with the feet together. The support is low, and the center of gravity is as close to the support (the feet) as possible. As the center of gravity is brought up to its normal place high, the supports return to their normal middle level. It is understood that a certain amount of raising the heels must take place in a deep knee bend. Any special use of the feet can be written in detail.

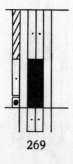

269

ANALYSIS OF DISTANCE

It will be noted in Fig. 268 that high for the center of gravity is
the length of the legs above the point of support, and low is the
length of the legs below the point of support. The length of the legs
is therefore used as a yard stick. Within the body, three such
lengths are established.

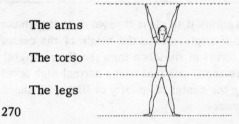

The arms

The torso

The legs

270

These lengths in the body are thought of much as step-lengths
in that there is the normal (or full) distance, as in a step; there is
a short distance and a very short distance. There is also a long
distance and a very long distance in relation to the point where the
weight is. Since we are most familiar with standing on the feet and
lowering the center of gravity to the floor, let us examine first the
in-between degrees that occur there.

Between place middle and place high there are two degrees of
lifting. The distance from place middle is analyzed in the same
way as the distance of a step. But whereas the distance of steps is
analyzed in terms of step lengths, we regard distance in the use of
the center of gravity in terms of body lengths.

	one length		one length
	small distance		small distance
	very small distance		very small distance
	in place		in place
271a		b	

Distance in a forward direction   Distance in an upward direction

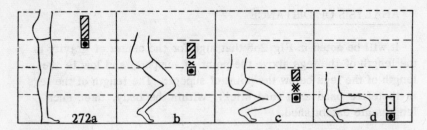

In the above diagrams it is clear that we describe distance according to the point of origin. Thus the height of the center of gravity is described in terms of distance from the floor: slightly lifted, lifted a short distance, or lifted to the normal high level. Whether you are lowering the center of gravity or lifting it, these are absolute points in space.

The height of jumps can also be indicated by the use of the center of gravity.

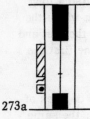 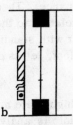 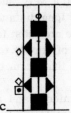 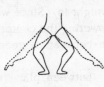

A high jump, higher than normal.

A very high jump (as off a springboard)

The center of gravity stays where it is; no rise.

Here we have an example of a hand stand. Note that the hand symbols are placed in the support column. The center of gravity is two body lengths from the point of support (the floor); hence, the double wide high direction. The legs are straight up from the hips.

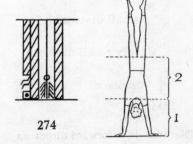

Falling flat on your face; that is, catching the weight on your hands at the last moment. The weight of the body travels forward and to middle level (the same level as the support). This results in the flat-as-a-board fall. The point of support is the feet on the floor and the center of gravity ends up horizontal and forward of that point.

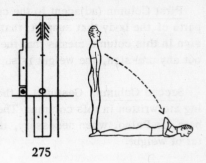

275

CLARIFICATIONS

OLD VERSION OF WRITING CENTER OF GRAVITY

Since you may encounter scores or printed materials of the past containing the old version of writing the level of the center of gravity, we will describe the method used formerly so that you can read the old notation correctly.

The chief difference in the old version was that the level of the center of gravity at the floor was low. Hence, in Fig. 275 above, the forward middle sign would have been a forward low sign.

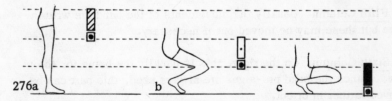

276a   b   c

Old version: The three levels of the center of gravity.

THE USE OF THE COLUMNS

Certain parts of the body have definite homes; that is, columns in which they belong. Whenever an identifying pre-sign is used, there is always the chance to make use of another column, if for some reason the regular one is crowded. Let us review quickly the use of the columns.

First Column (adjacent to the center line). This is reserved for parts of the body that support; that is, carry the weight. Any body sign in this column means that the part is acting as a support. Without any pre-sign, the weight is supported on both feet.

Second Column. Gestures of the whole leg and the parts of the leg are written in this column. The single hip can also be written here, and also, when necessary, the lowering or lifting of the center of weight.

Third Column. On the right side this is reserved for tilting and rotating the chest. Other movements of the chest are also written here, but the appropriate chest pre-sign must be used. On the left side, the third column is used for the pelvic girdle and the whole torso. For each, the pre-sign is used. The shoulder may be written here. When there is room, the parts of the leg may be written out in the third column, but this should be avoided as much as possible.

Fourth Column. This is reserved for the whole arm and also for the parts of the arm. Special movements of the lower arm, hands, and fingers are written in the next column out, additional columns being used where need be.

Fifth Column. Usually the movements of the hand are written here but these may be moved out if necessary.

Sixth Column. On the right, this is usually the home for the head. Since the head pre-signs are always used, this part can be moved farther in or out.

Additional Signs on the Right of the Staff. Way signs are placed on the right, beyond indications for the head. Prop columns can be on either side, but more often are placed on the right. The same is true of auxiliary floor columns.

Additional Signs on the Left of the Staff. The stage direction pins are written on the left beyond any movement indications for the body. The numbering of the bars and of the counts, when used, is also placed outside on the left.

PART TWO

Part One of this book has treated the basic areas of movement notation in considerable detail. The following chapters deal in more general terms with the more intricate and advanced movement problems. They will give the student an idea of how these problems are handled in Labanotation, will demonstrate the scope of the system, and for the advanced student and the professional will be a useful reference source. A later volume will provide detailed treatment of these problems.

CHAPTER XI

Subtleties of Movement

SHIFT OF WEIGHT

The stepping into open positions of the feet and from open positions into closed positions was discussed somewhat briefly in Chapter IV. To write these actions directly and simply, we described the use of the staple. By this device the transitions into and from open positions could be easily noted without the need for exact analysis of the actual placement of the weight and the use of timing and levels. The emphasis at that point was on writing the resulting position. For more advanced work, it is important that the movement itself, and not just the final result, be recorded, and so here we discuss the problem more fully.

Two things must be clearly understood in the writing of shifts of weight. First, we must understand where the direction place is.

Place is beneath your center of weight.

See "Where is Place?" in Chapter I. In stating the direction place in a movement description, the writer is apt to refer to a direction other than true place; that is, a direction into which the center of gravity travels and which thus becomes the subsequent place position, but which is not place at the start of the movement.

Second, we must understand why the writing of these shifts poses any problem at all. To see this, we must recognize the dual function of the support column when open positions are being written. Note the path of the center of weight in these notations:

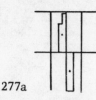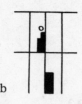

277a
b
c

| The center of weight moves forward by means of a step on the left leg. | The center of weight moves forward by means of leaping onto the left leg. | The center of weight moves forward by means of a jump on both legs. |

In each case, at the end of the movement, the weight is directly above the supports.

In the figure to the right, the center of weight does not move at all. What has moved are the supports which now have a different relation to the center; that is, the right leg is supporting to the right and the left to the left. In this case, the support columns do not tell us where the center of weight has traveled, but rather the relation of the two supports to the center. Since each leg had an equal pull, the center did not move.

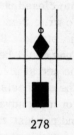

278

In stepping into and out of open positions, we have to consider not only the new relation of the supports to the center but also the path, even though it is small, of the center of weight. We must then be very clear as to what the symbols in the support column are telling us.

STEPPING INTO OPEN POSITIONS

To step into an open position, one foot remains in its original direction (place) while the other steps out. The center of weight travels in the direction of the leading leg. However, since part of the weight is retained on the passive leg, the center travels only half the distance of a normal step. When the movement is completed, the center of weight is directly between the two supports; hence, the direction "place" has moved in a like manner.

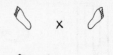

Stepping out with the right
foot. In this example, ×
marks the center of weight.

279

If there is no change in level, either the direction symbol (place)
is written or a hold sign is used. However, when a change in level
must be shown, a direction symbol must be used, since level is not
indicated by a hold sign.

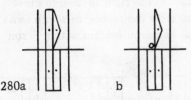

Stepping from first position into
second with the right leg. The
left holds its original position.

Stepping from first posi-
tion into fourth with a
change of level.

Once the position is established, any further change in level is
indicated by writing that position in the new level.

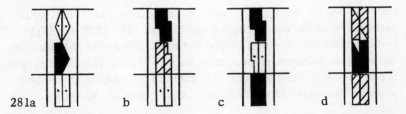

Note the difference between writing the movement into an open position and any subsequent statement of that same position.

STEPPING INTO CLOSED POSITIONS

In order to close the feet when standing in an open position, the
weight must first be transferred to one foot before the other can free
itself in order to close in. There are two distinct actions: 1) shifting of the weight; 2) bringing the other foot into place.

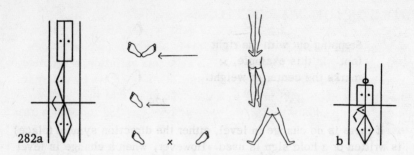

282a   x   b

Shifting from second position into first, closing to the left. The weight must shift to the left foot before the right is free to close into first. The shift of weight also tells the reader to which foot he should close. Fig. (b) shows the same movement with a faster transition.

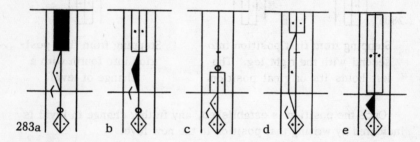

283a   b   c   d   e

Here are shown several variations in the performance of one basic pattern. Note the use of timing and levels. The shift of weight from an open position to a closed one can occur before the beat, on the beat, or be extended over more than one beat. The same-part-of-the-body bow is used to show that the foot onto which the weight shifts is the same as the previous support; that is, it does not move.

In certain instances where a direction other than place is used, the shift of weight is understood and so need not be written. However, it is a good rule to write in the shift whenever a doubt might exist or where exactness of performance is required. In the examples to the right, a shift to the left foot is understood.

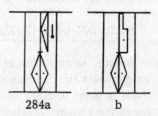

284a   b

DIRECTION VARIATIONS

As a rule, the basic directions and levels serve our purpose in describing movement. However, where a precise variation is required, an in-between direction must be written. This is shown by two main direction symbols separated by a dot. To show that they are one unit in timing and direction, the two symbols are tied together with a bow.

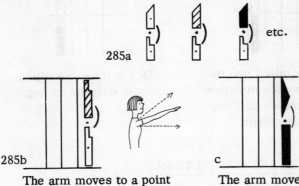

285a etc.

285b

The arm moves to a point
between forward middle
and forward high.

c

The arm moves to a point
between place low
and side low.

An in-between direction may lie
between three main directions.
Here, the arm gestures to a point
midway between three points:

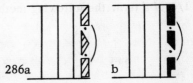

286a b

If a part of the body has already moved into one of the directions, it is not necessary to repeat the direction symbol; only the dot and the next direction symbol need be shown.

Both arms start
side horizontal.
The right lifts
half way to side
high; the left
lowers half way
to side low.

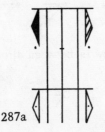

287a

The chest
starts place
high and then
moves half way
to side high. It
then returns to
place high.

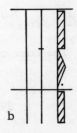

b

If the connecting bow is not used, two movements are indicated; the first into the first direction stated and the second half way into the following direction.

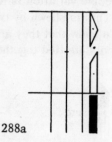

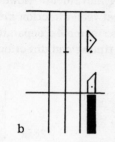

288a

b

The arm is raised into the diagonal middle direction and then moves half way to side middle.

This is the same action with different timing.

IN-BETWEEN DEGREES OF TURN

Finer distinctions may be needed in the amount of turn one performs or the direction one faces on stage in order to give the right expression to a gesture or position. In order to describe less than 1/8 of a turn, the following method is used:

289

$\boxed{\vee} = 1/16$

The degree to be indicated lies directly between the two pins written.

290

$\angle - 3/16$ $\prec - 5/16$ etc.

The same method is used to show in-between directions on stage.

291   etc.

RELATIONSHIP PINS - POSITION SIGNS

The relationship pins have been used only in a general way until now. Their use can be more specific. In addition to showing the direction of the relationship, in front of, to the side of, they can also indicate the level - above, below, in front of and slightly above, to the right of and slightly below, and the like. This is the complete table of relationship pins:

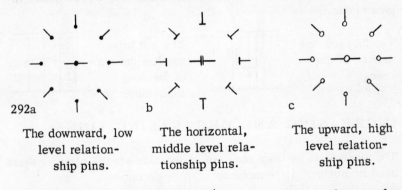

292a	b	c
The downward, low level relationship pins.	The horizontal, middle level relationship pins.	The upward, high level relationship pins.

The sign for below can be written ∮ or ─●─ . This is also true for above: ∮ or ─○─ , and for center: ╪ or ─╫─ .

Note. To avoid any confusion between the high relationship pins and the white pins used for stage direction signs, remember that the relationship pins are always placed as close as possible to the movement which they describe, whereas the stage direction pins are drawn larger and are placed away from the staff on the left.

FOR THE ARMS

The pins are used to show the relation of the arms to one another or to the body. This means that, although the arms are held in the position indicated by the direction symbol, their extremities (the fingertips) are held in the position indicated by the pin.

The arms (that is, their extremities) are in front of the body.

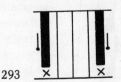

293

The right lower arm is horizontally in front of the left.   294a

The right arm is above the left.   b

FOR TOUCHING

The contact between different parts of the body can be shown in greater detail.

The foot touches in back of the knee.   295a

The left hand touches the top of the head from above.   b

INCREASING AND DECREASING SIGNS

The symbols to indicate increase or decrease are the same as those used in music: $\bigvee$ - increase; $\bigwedge$ - decrease.

The quality or other aspect of movement to be increased or decreased is placed within the open end of the symbol.

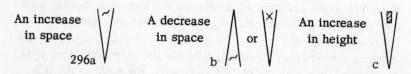

An increase in space   296a

A decrease in space   b   or

An increase in height   c

A decrease in space may be regarded from two points of view - as a lessening of width or as an increase in narrowness. The choice of description will rest on the emphasis desired in the movement.

The symbol is placed alongside the sequence which it describes.

The leaps are shown to become increasingly wide.   297

The repeated arm movement becomes increasingly high. No exact result is stated.   298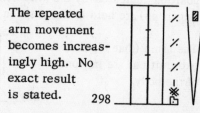

THE HANDS

The symbol ⧊ represents the whole hand and is used whenever a general description is required. For a more specific analysis, the hand is divided into its component parts: the palm and the fingers. The movement categories applicable to hand movements are: directional movements, contacting, facing (for the palm), stretching and flexing, and spreading and closing in (of the fingers).

THE WHOLE HAND

As we saw in Chapter IX, movements of the hand in space are written by using the directional symbols. Like the whole arm, the hand can also flex and stretch. It is normally held with a slight curve through the palm and fingers.

Stretching the Whole Hand. The hand has two degrees of stretching:

Straight (flat)   Convex (arched)

299a   b

Flexing the Whole Hand. The hand has six degrees of flexing. These range from a slightly flexed hand to a tightly closed fist. The thumb closes in opposition to the fingers, ending above them.

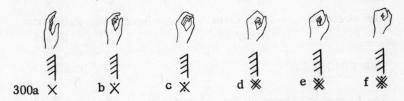

300a X   b X   c X   d X   e X   f X

Note the difference in description between placing the flex or stretch symbol before or after the hand symbol.

The stretched hand moves up.

301a

The hand stretches. (The duration line shows the timing of the action.)

b

THE PALM

The palms of the hands are often used to give expression to a gesture. The symbol for the palm is ꔆ . Note that it is drawn long and thin, not square, and with the bottom side left open.

Facing of the Palm. The palm sign, like the other boxed symbols, faces the direction placed after it. It does not, like a limb, move into the direction.

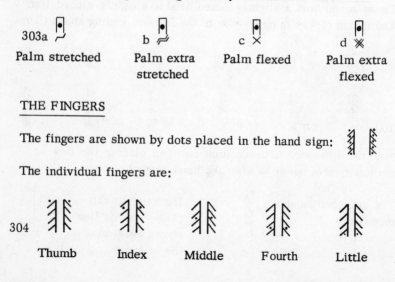

302a	b	c	d
Palm faces forward.	Palm faces down.	Palm faces up.	Palm faces back.

The Back of the Hand. The reverse of the palm is the back of the hand: ꔆ . The white circle in the center indicates the back just as the black circle in the center of the palm sign indicates the inner side. The back of the hand is not usually used for movement but for touching or as guidance in a gesture.

Stretching and Flexing the Palm. The palm alone can be stretched and flexed. This means that the action is centered in the palm with the fingers being scarcely affected.

303a	b	c	d
Palm stretched	Palm extra stretched	Palm flexed	Palm extra flexed

THE FINGERS

The fingers are shown by dots placed in the hand sign:

The individual fingers are:

304				
Thumb	Index	Middle	Fourth	Little

Stretching and Flexing the Fingers.   Movements of the fingers scarcely affect the palm at all. The fingers can stretch or flex without an accompanying movement in the palm.

305a   Straight fingers

b   Extended fingers

c   Flexed fingers

d   Very flexed fingers

Below are two fairly common combinations of the separate use of the fingers and of the palm.

306a =

Cupped palm, extended fingers.

b =

Closed fingers, extended palm.

A hand position can be shown by describing the use of the individual fingers.

307 =

Spreading and Closing the Fingers.   The fingers can be separated and spread, as well as closed in, and pressed together. The symbols for spread and close are:

308a   ⌣ =   Slightly spread

b   ⌣ =   Very spread

c   △ =   Closed

d   △ =   Tightly closed

Note that the symbols △ and ⌣ are related to the × and ⌐ symbols, since these actions are similar though they occur in a different plane.

309a

A claw is produced by both flexing and spreading the fingers.

b

The "V" for victory hand gesture.

PARTNER WORK

In recording work involving partners or objects, the notator must know how to indicate grasping and carrying. The most important aspects of this very detailed range of movement are discussed here.

THE CONTACT SIGNS

310a   b   c

     Near   Touching   Grasping

      d   e

Carrying, taking the weight.   Carrying with a grasp, holding.

Contact Between Parts of the Body.

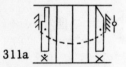   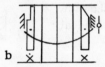   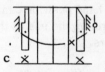

311a   b   c

The right hand is just above the left wrist.	The right hand touches the left wrist from above.	The right hand grasps the left wrist from above.

Grasping. In grasping, no weight is taken over; merely the act of grasping occurs. The × is placed next to the active part.

312a   b   c

The right hand grasps the left.	The left hand grasps the right.	Both grasp equally.

Supporting a Partner. In partner work, the grasping and lifting often occur around the waist. Other parts of the body may also support. To designate which part, we use the following modifications of the body signs:

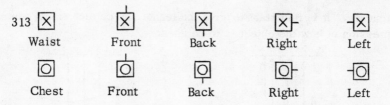

313 Waist   Front   Back   Right   Left

Chest   Front   Back   Right   Left

In the same way, the different sides of the whole torso and of the pelvic girdle can be shown.

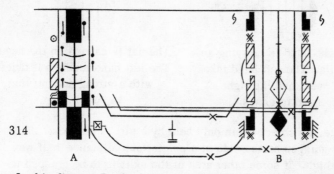

314

A   B

In this figure, B, the boy, stands behind A, the girl. His hands support her through grasping, thus indicating the lift. Note that the lines for contact must be drawn where they interfere least with the rest of the notation. For this reason, they may be swung lower down or swung upwards, if need be. The extremities of the lines indicate the timing of the movement.

Contact Between Part of the Body and an Object.   When an object such as a stick, basket, or article of clothing is used in a dance, a simplified drawing of this object is placed near the dance staff, usually on the right. The object is given a column, so that there is no need to repeat the drawing. An index to all objects used during a score should appear at the beginning or end.

315

Chair   Table   Sword   Fan

To indicate contact with an object, the contact line should be placed as closely as possible to the part of the object that is being touched. It is important to give the reader the correct visual impression of how the object is to be used.

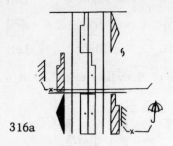

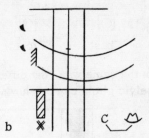

316a

b

The right hand is carrying an umbrella. The left hand takes it over, and the right hand releases.

The hat is carried on the head. The left hand touches it twice, with a strong accent; that is, with a tap.

In dance, an object commonly held by a girl is the skirt. This is usually grasped at the side at a comfortable distance half way down the thigh. If some other area of the skirt is to be grasped it can be indicated by the use of small direction symbols which relate to the front, back, up and down of the skirt itself. A simplified drawing of a skirt can be used in the object column, or merely the word "skirt" can be written.

317a

b

The lower edge is grasped.

The front center section is grasped.

Usually carrying is accomplished through grasping; that is, through closing the hand or limb. Some objects, however, can be carried through stretching, as, for instance, spreading the fingers inside a jug.

The contact line can be swung above (as here) or below, depending on how the object is carried.

318

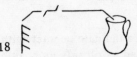

THE ADDRESSING SIGN

A gesture may be directed toward a person or an object which may be some distance away. To indicate this special directing of a motion, the addressing sign is used.

This sign is drawn from the active person's column out to the right. The line begins at the part of the body doing the addressing; if it is the whole body, the line is drawn right through the staff. The line ends in a curve, within which is placed the sign for the person or object being addressed.

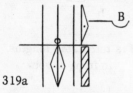

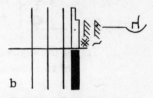

319a
An arm gesture directed
toward a person - B

b
Pointing to the chair

MEETING

The meeting line is a stroke placed on the right of the staff at the point where the dancer whose movements are written within the staff meets another dancer. The stroke describes the position of the person met.

320a
A is in front.

b
A is on your right.

c
A is diagonally in front.

Although this meeting is often indicated in the accompanying floor plans, there is occasionally a need to state it next to the movement pattern. Note the relationship of A and B in the example below.

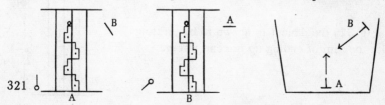
321

DISTANCE SIGN

Gauging distance on stage - to indicate traveling jumps, for example - is done in terms of step lengths. The number of step lengths is placed within a box to the right of the staff. The sign is also used to indicate the spatial relationship of two dancers.

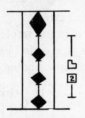

322a

b

Travel the equivalent
of two steps.

B is three step lengths
in front of you.

STAGE AREA SIGNS

The area on stage used by the dancer can be indicated by special signs. These are used apart from the stage plans, and are particularly useful when the destination on stage of a particular path must be indicated.

323a
Front center
stage area

b
Right front
stage area

c
Right stage
area

d
Center stage

To the right are examples of the use of the stage area sign in the starting position.

324

In Fig. 325 the dancer is shown to be circling with the aim of ending up in center stage.

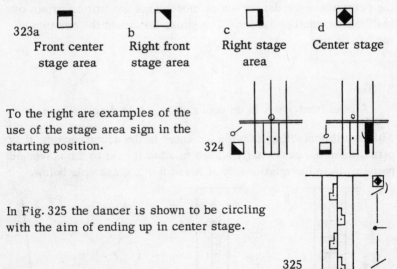

325

DYNAMICS

Dynamics - the quality and texture of movement - can be described in fine detail in Labanotation through the use of effort signs. Here, however, only a general indication is given, sufficiently useful for ordinary purposes.

INNATE DYNAMICS

Patterns of movement contain certain innate dynamics which are often performed unconsciously. For example, high steps are lighter; low steps heavier. Timing of a movement can change the dynamics. In a movement where the body must cover a great deal of space in a short time, there will be an inevitable increase in the use of energy. A change in dynamics can be seen in jumps performed at too slow or too rapid a tempo. In a swinging motion, the body makes use of the force of gravity so that the motion is speeded up as it approaches the downward direction and slows up as it approaches the upward direction, as these examples show:

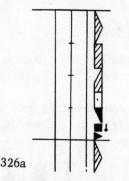

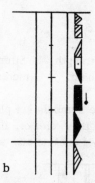

326a

b

Swing in which the pull of gravity is utilized. There is a natural slowing up as the arm rises.

This timing requires a controlled lowering of the arm and an additional use of energy in order to speed up at the end.

The effect of musical accompaniment on movement in terms of dynamics must not be overlooked. The same movement sequences will be performed with different dynamic qualities when danced to different pieces of music. This will be so in spite of the fact that the same tempi and metric structures are present in each piece.

STRENGTH AND LIGHTNESS

In the case of innate dynamics no special signs are needed because the changes in the use of energy occur naturally. In other cases, however, it is necessary to write these changes. We indicate the use or the absence of energy with the following signs:

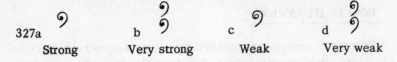

327a   b   c   d

  Strong   Very strong   Weak   Very weak

These signs are similar to the light and strong accent signs - ♪ and ♭. But whereas the accents are used for quick movement, the dynamic signs can be given a duration line to indicate the persistence of the energy, or a hold sign to indicate that the energy is held, or an increasing sign (crescendo) or a diminishing sign to show that the energy is increased or decreased.

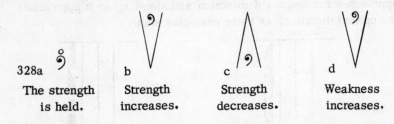

328a   b   c   d

The strength   Strength   Strength   Weakness

is held.   increases.   decreases.   increases.

These symbols are placed inside the columns of the body parts to which they refer or, if the description is for the entire body, they are placed outside and drawn much larger.

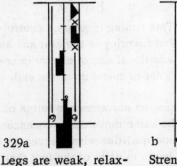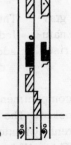

329a   b   c

Legs are weak, relax-   Strength in the   Whole body action is

ed, during the steps.   legs is held.   strong, then weak.

TREMOLO, TRILL

A small, wavy line is used to indicate vibrating, trembling, or shaking. These actions can be further clarified by using the dynamic signs with the wavy line.

Strong vibration

Weak vibration

330a   b

In a shaking motion it may also be necessary to show the direction of the shaking. This is done by using the relationship pins to indicate very small movements in space.

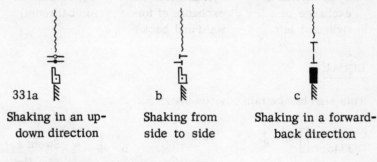

331a

Shaking in an up-down direction

b

Shaking from side to side

c

Shaking in a forward-back direction

ACCELERANDO AND RITARDANDO

It is possible to speed up or to slow down a movement into a single direction. This is shown by writing the same symbol twice and indicating the change in timing by their different lengths. The symbols are connected by a bow.

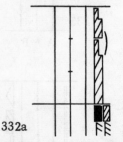

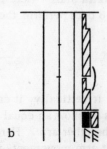

332a

b

The gesture starts slowly and becomes more rapid.

The gesture starts quickly and then gradually peters out.

THE ANALOGY SIGNS

Analogy signs are sometimes used in scores, but generally speaking they are used only as aids to quick writing. In a finished score, the notation should be written out in full. The analogy symbols are:

333a   ====

b   ~)

Equal   Similar to

333c   ⌣

d   ⟨

e   ⟨⌣

Symmetrical in
exchange of
right and left

Symmetrical in
exchange of for-
ward and back

Opposition (as
in ballroom)

EQUAL

This sign has certain obvious uses:

334a   [] = ♩

b   ↓ = Sword

As an indication of timing

As an indication of an object

It can also be used to show that one dancer does the same as another, thus avoiding the use of an extra staff. Here it indicates that A and B both perform the notated sequence.

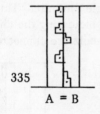

335

A = B

By placing it vertically, it can be used for rough notes to show an equal (parallel) movement for the other arm. Here it indicates that the left arm movements parallel those of the right.

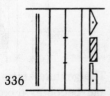

336

SIMILAR

This symbol is used more frequently in scores, since it indicates freedom in interpretation or ad libbing.

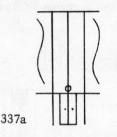

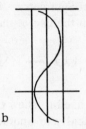

337a The ad lib. sign for the arms only.

b Ad lib. signs across the staff indicate freedom to improvise.

A movement pattern can be indicated and then followed by this similar sign to express continuous movement in the same general vein.

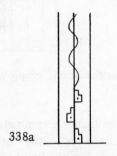

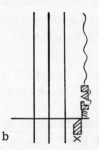

338a An ad lib. run

b Continuous arm movements on this order

Ad Lib. for Timing. To indicate an ad lib. for timing, the sign is modified thus: ⟨

This sign is used wherever an exact performance in timing is not required or where only a general indication of the timing has been given. The sign is placed outside the staff on the right.

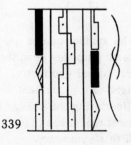

339

SYMMETRICAL

There are two possibilities for symmetrical patterns.

Lateral Symmetry. This sign indicates the exchange of right
and left in the use of the body and of space.

340   ⊔ —   ◁=▷,   ◫=◫,   ◫=◫,   ◫=◫

It can be used to show that one person moves
symmetrically to another. In the example
here A performs the sequence written while B
moves symmetrically to A.

341

A B

It can be used in rough notes to indicate symmetrical arm movements. Here the left arm
performs a pattern symmetrical to that being
done by the right arm.

342

A mirror image, in which one person faces the other, employs
this form of symmetry.

Forward-Backward Symmetry. This sign indicates a symmetry
in which there is an exchange of forward and back and of the direction of turning. It appears more rarely in dance, but can be used in
the same way as the sign for lateral symmetry.

343   Ɛ —   ◫=◫,   ◫=◫,   ◫=◫,   ▷=▷

The symbol can be used for the
same purposes described above
for lateral symmetry. To the
right is a movement sequence
illustrating the change in movement that takes place as a result
of this symmetry.   344

becomes

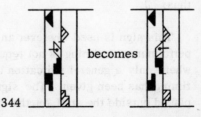

OPPOSITION

By opposition we mean the combined use of both forms of symmetry as the symbol itself suggests: $\mathcal{E}\omega$. Opposition is used most frequently in ballroom dancing. The sign indicates the following exchange:

345 $\quad \mathcal{E}\omega \; - \; \triangleleft\!=\!\triangleright, \quad \square\!=\!\square, \quad \square\!=\!\square, \quad \square\!=\!\square$

Note that in this case the turn is in the same direction.

As with the other analogy signs, the opposition sign is used to eliminate the need of a second staff in writing. In any dance in which the use of opposition appears only briefly, it should be written out in full. The use of the symbol is permissible, however, in pieces which are basically in the nature of ballroom dances. In the example here, A performs the pattern written; B moves in opposition.

346

CONTINUATION BOW

When a symbol must be carried over from the end of one staff to the beginning of another, a small vertical bow is used to indicate the continuance of the movement.

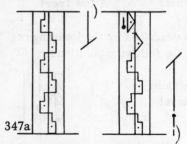

347a

The way sign is continued into the next staff.

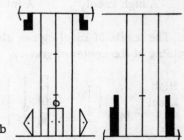

b

The arm gesture to forward low starts at the end of the previous staff and continues in the following measure on the next staff.

CHAPTER XII

Kneeling, Sitting, Lying

SUPPORTING ON THE KNEES

In the question of supporting the weight on parts of the body other than the feet, supporting on the knees is obviously the first situation to consider. Kneeling is comparable to supporting on the feet, both in the use of levels and in the use of the lower leg in a similar manner to the foot.

LEVELS OF KNEELING

348a A high kneel   b A middle kneel   c A low kneel

The levels of kneeling can also be described by the lowering or raising of the center of gravity. Note the following positions:

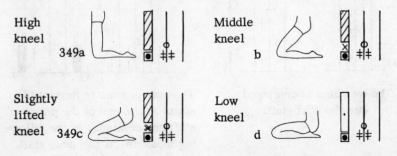

High kneel 349a

Middle kneel b

Slightly lifted kneel 349c

Low kneel d

The choice of description - the level of the support, or the use of the center of gravity - will depend on the content of the movement.

One thing should be made clear. When the support is on the knees, the level of the center of gravity is judged from that standpoint. When the weight is on the feet, the level of the center of gravity is taken from the normal standing position (the one with which you are already familiar). Thus, high level for the center of gravity in kneeling is the same as half way down toward the floor when you are standing on your feet.

350

By writing the level of the knee support, we give a direct description of the level, and any subsequent step onto the foot will bring the center of weight into its normal standing position. If, instead, the center of gravity has been written in kneeling movements, you must indicate its eventual return to normal.

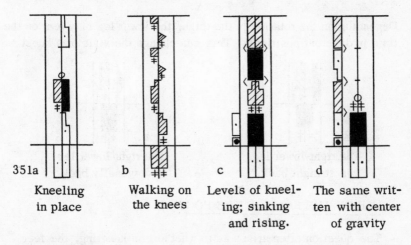

351a Kneeling in place

b Walking on the knees

c Levels of kneeling; sinking and rising.

d The same written with center of gravity

In Fig. (a) the plié on the supporting leg is deep enough to allow kneeling on the left. Watch for an ordinary step on the foot after kneeling supports. Note the use of the bow for the same part of the body in (c) and (d). It is not always necessary to write the direction of a knee support when it is obvious, as in (d).

Shift of weight is the same on the
knees as on the feet. The use of open
positions is identical. Position writing
is used, with the staple indicating the
support which does not move, or the
movement notation for shift of weight
is written out.

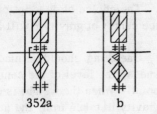

352a   b

PLACEMENT OF THE LOWER LEG

In a high kneel, the weight is on the knees, but the lower leg
rests on the floor in order to maintain balance. This is understood
and so is not written. However, there may be a definite placement
of the lower leg necessary to the choreography and this must be
indicated.

353a   b

Depending on the rotation in the thigh, the lower leg may rest on the
floor in different positions. This can change the style of a kneel.

354a   b

The right lower leg   The right lower leg
is straight back.   is diagonally back.

USE OF THE BALL OF THE FOOT

The question often arises as to whether, in kneeling, the feet
should be tucked under - that is, the ball of the foot touching the
floor - or whether the feet should be extended with the instep touching the floor. Generally speaking, it is not necessary to indicate
this, since the choice will usually depend on the degree of comfort
rather than on any choreographic necessity. However, there are

times when it is important to indicate the position because the subsequent movement may be affected.

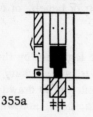 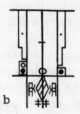

355a

The feet are tucked under in order to prepare for transferring
weight onto the feet and
standing up.

The instep is resting on the
floor in preparation for sinking back to the floor.

Note: The symbol ⊠ means the top of the foot when it appears
in the leg column.

SITTING

The novice's way of learning to fall is to go through the stages of
kneeling, sitting, and lying in quick succession. Sitting is often
an intermediate stage in lowering the body to the floor or in rising
from the floor. There are, of course, other ways of getting down to
the floor, such as falling onto the hands, leaning over and taking
the weight on one hand and thus lowering the body. Whatever the
means, a few things must be clearly indicated in writing the movement: either the transition from feet to knees to hips (this usually
takes care of the lowering of the center of gravity) or, where levels
of kneeling are not used, the lowering of the center of gravity.
Writing the body at floor level is unfamiliar at first, and care should
be taken to tell the reader all he needs to know but without cumbersome detail.

LEVELS ON THE FLOOR

The hips support at middle level; there is no high or low support
on the floor. A high or low support would be possible if one were
working with props or aerial acrobatics, for example, but this is a
distinct movement area which will be investigated later.

Once the body has been lowered to floor level, the legs can no longer perform low gestures; they can only be horizontal (middle level) or high. If you were sitting on a chair or bench, of course, low leg gestures would still be possible.

In sitting, it is taken for granted that the legs rest on the floor and this contact need not be written. When it is necessary to indicate that the limbs touch the floor, a straight line is drawn from the leg column into the support column. The toe, heel, and whole foot hooks are used when those specific parts are involved, the straight line being neutral, so to speak.

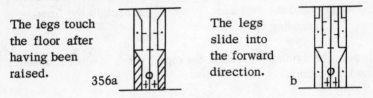

The legs touch the floor after having been raised. 356a

The legs slide into the forward direction. b

WAYS OF SITTING DOWN ON THE FLOOR

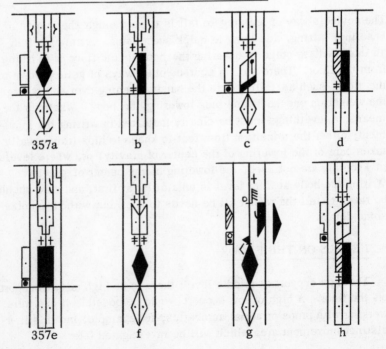

357a   b   c   d

357e   f   g   h

LYING ON THE FLOOR

When the whole torso symbol is used in the support column, it is
usually placed on one side or the other, it doesn't matter which.
If it were placed dead center, it would be hard to see whether there
is a pin attached to signify supporting on the back or on the front,
for the heavy center line of the staff would hide it. This is also
true of the individual chest and pelvic girdle signs. Lying can also
be indicated by using the hip and shoulder signs. When these are
used as a starting position, direction symbols must also be shown
to make clear whether the position is prone or supine.

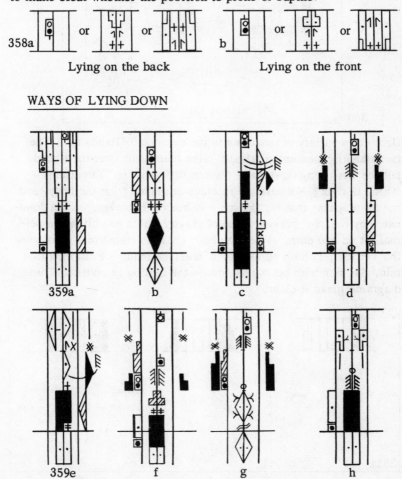

358a or   or   b   or   or

Lying on the back   Lying on the front

WAYS OF LYING DOWN

359a   b   c   d

359e   f   g   h

ANALYSIS OF DIRECTION

360

"HANDS UP!"

Here are a variety of reactions to the command "Hands up!" The two standing men automatically raise their arms over their heads, but the two lying down have chosen different "up" directions. Which is right? Normally, directions are taken from the body, and not from space; that is, the room or stage. However, we are dominated by the ever-present force of gravity which establishes a permanent up and down. When the body changes its normal relation to the vertical, certain adjustments must be made. Following this rule, the man with his hands toward the ceiling is correct. These diagrams make it clear:

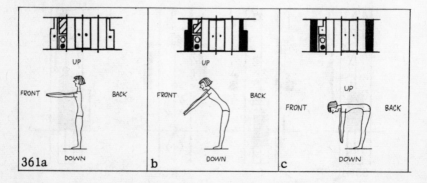

361a   b   c

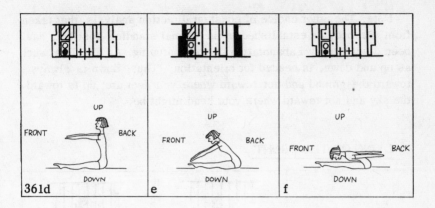

LYING ON THE BACK

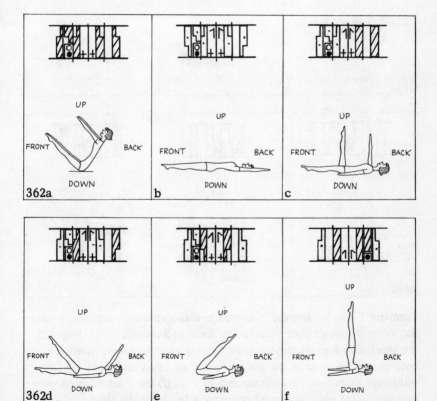

Note: The other choice of constant direction analysis, that taken from the body as established in the normal standing position, has been discarded by Labanotation as too confusing. An absolute, such as up and down, is needed for orientation. Thus, down is always toward the ground and not toward where your feet are; up is toward the sky and not toward where your head might be.

LYING ON THE FRONT

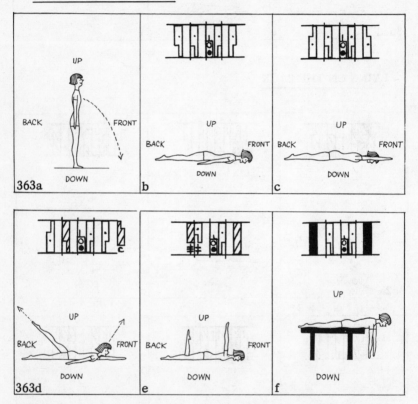

Compare Figs. (a) and (b) to notice how the space directions remain the same although your relation to them has changed. In Fig. (d) the head may feel as though it is moving in a backward direction, but, as can be seen in the diagram, it has lifted only into the forward high direction. As illustrated in Fig. (f) the limbs can move in a low level when the point of support is above the floor.

LYING ON THE SIDE

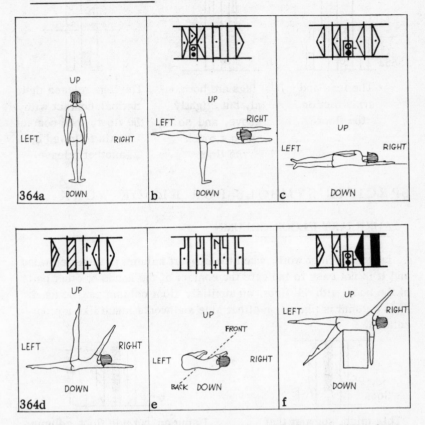

Since up and down are constant, you need only find out where front
and back are, then right and left will fall into place. One easy way
to determine front is to give a quick command: "Get up and run forward!" People will automatically go into the right direction without
having time to think. This test works whether you are lying on your
front, side, or back.

LIMBS CONTACTING THE FLOOR

It is understood in lying on the floor that the limbs rest on the
floor unless some other indication is given for them. If a limb is
to be held horizontally just clear of the floor, this can be shown
either by an above sign or by using the release sign.

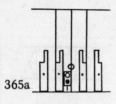 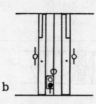

365a	b	c
The legs and arms rest on the floor.	The legs are horizontal, but slightly above, and so do not touch the floor.	The legs release their normal contact with the floor, then contact again followed by another release.

SPECIFIC SYMBOLS FOR FLOOR WORK

AUXILIARY FLOOR COLUMN

In writing floor work, when the support column is rather crowded and it is not easy to indicate the contact of the hands or other parts of the body with the floor, an auxiliary floor column can be used. This column is placed on either side and works much like a prop column.

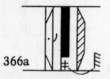

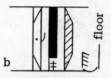

366a	b
This might suggest that the hand touches the knee.	Using an outside floor column makes the contact entirely clear.

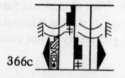

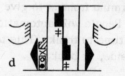

366c	d
It is difficult to indicate the sliding of the hands while the support columns are being used.	The same sequence is easily written through using an auxiliary floor column. In a simple case like this, the floor column is understood because of the context of the movement.

SOLE OF THE FOOT

The symbols for the sole and for the top of the foot are the same as for the palm and for the back of the hand.

367a **Sole or palm**   b **Back of hand or top of foot**

As long as each appears in its own column, there is no confusion. Instances where special identification is needed occur when the palm sign must appear in the support column or where a specific foot sign cannot be placed in the leg column and must be written elsewhere. In these cases the following identifications are used:

368a   Palm of the hand   b   Sole of the foot

(See glossary for other signs related to the hand or foot area sign.)

SPOT HOLD

A spot hold ⊗ is used when a part of the body retains its contact with a certain spot. This spot may be on the floor, on a prop - such as a chair or a tree - or on another person. It is stronger than a space hold from which the symbol is derived because, when using a space hold, the dancer can travel in space while maintaining a certain space relation with one part of the body. In a spot hold, he is tied down to that spot. To remember it, think of × marking the spot.

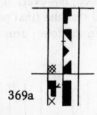

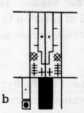

369a

The left toe has a spot hold during the hops on the right foot.

The feet have a spot hold while the hips slide back.

CHAPTER XIII

Rotations of the Limbs

ROTATIONS OF THE ARM

The symbols ◊ and ◊ have been used to show turns of the whole body, such as pivot turns or turns in the air. This is their meaning when placed in the support column; they describe the support and its effect on the whole body.

The same symbols are also used for other parts of the body to describe rotations or twists. Each part has its own range of ability to rotate, some being more flexible than others.

ROTATIONS OF THE WHOLE ARM

The whole arm rotates in the shoulder joint. The shoulder area should not be affected; that is, there should be no displacement in the shoulder blade. The arm moves in one piece; however, if a great deal of rotation is desired, it will be found that the final part of the rotation occurs in the extremity; that is, in the lower arm and the hand.

Placement of the Symbol. When no other movement occurs, the rotation sign is placed in the arm column, as in Fig. (a). However, rotations often occur as the arms are moving in space, and so, when need be, they can be written alongside and are linked to the arm column by a small horizontal bow, as in (b).

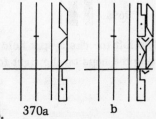

370a   b

Cancellation of a Rotation. A previous rotation is retained until another rotation occurs or a back-to-normal sign is written.

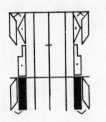

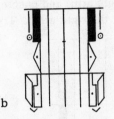

371a

b

The arms are carried forward inturned and rotate out as they are carried to the side.

The arms remain rotated out as they move to the side and then return to normal as they are brought down.

Amount of Rotation. The amount of rotation can be indicated by the degree of twisting that occurs, 1/8, 1/4, 1/2, and so on. As explained in Chapter XI, the description can also be done in terms of where the palm faces. Often the amount of rotation is unimportant - the reader is left free to do as much as the movement demands or as he feels inclined - and the rotation sign is left blank.

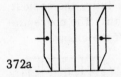

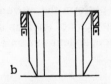

372a

b

c

Rotate the arms out 1/4 turn.

Rotate the arms out until the palms face up.

Rotate the arms out as far as possible or as desired.

Determining Direction of Rotation. When the arms are moving in low or horizontal planes, it is easy to see and feel which is an outward rotation and which is inward. However, when the arm is held high overhead, a seeming contradiction takes place. What was an outward rotation now appears to be an inward rotation, and vice versa. Where, before, the symbol for a rotation to the right would have been used, it now appears that it should be one to the left. Often the arm must be lowered in order to determine which is the direction of the rotation. One solution which works for the average right-handed person is to remember that, thanks to the standardization of the making of jars, light bulbs, radiator caps, and the like, the act of screwing is a rotation to the right (outward for the right arm) and unscrewing is a rotation to the left (inward rotation for the right arm). Try the examples below:

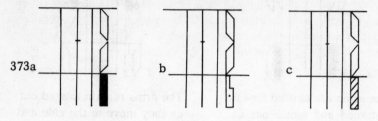

373a   b   c

ROTATIONS OF THE ELBOW

In the true sense of the word, the elbow cannot rotate; it can, however, activate a rotary movement in the center of the arm. This rotation takes place through the upper and lower part of the arm while the extremities, the shoulder and the hand, remain quiet. This movement appears in Oriental dance and also in other styles in a less exaggerated form. The term "lifting the elbows," used in ballet for the correct carriage of the arms, is actually a slight rotation of this kind. To perform the movement fully, the easiest way is to grasp a stationary object such as a chair. The concentration can then be on the independent movement of the elbow.

Grasping a chair and rotating the elbow in and out 374a

A simple ballet arm position

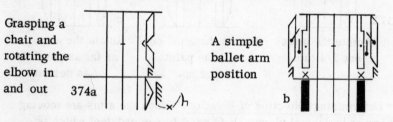

b

ROTATIONS OF THE LOWER ARM

The lower arm rotates from the elbow down. The hand is used merely as an extension of the lower arm and has no importance of its own. Note Fig. (b), where the lower arm rotation causes the hand to move in space.

375a   b

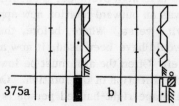

ROTATIONS OF THE HAND

As an isolated part, the hand cannot rotate. What we call a rotation of the hand is actually a rotation through the lower arm. However, the emphasis or motivation is in the hand - the extremity - and so by describing this as a hand rather than a lower arm rotation we give it a different expression. In addition, the hand is used with more sensitivity when a rotation is attributed to it.

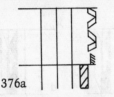

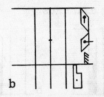

376a — Quick rotations of the hand overhead. The amount of rotation is unimportant.

b — Degree of rotation can be indicated where there is a need to be specific.

Circles of the Hand. Circles of the hand are usually a combination of a path in space plus a rotation. The rotation allows for a greater range of movement.

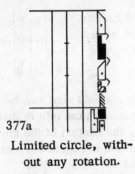

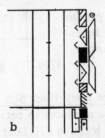

377a — Limited circle, without any rotation.

b — The circle is augmented by the use of rotations.

ROTATIONS OF THE LEG

ROTATED GESTURES OF THE WHOLE LEG

Rotations of the legs are very similar to rotations of the arms. The chief exceptions are that the legs are less flexible and hence more limited in range of motion and that they can rotate while supporting the body.

Placement of the Symbol. A rotation symbol in the leg gesture column means a rotation of the whole leg moving in the hip socket. In writing a rotation that occurs during a leg gesture, the rotation symbol is placed after the direction symbol and the two are tied to indicate the simultaneous action. The rotation can also be written in the third column when there is no body movement. In this case, it must be made clear that the rotation sign refers to the leg gesture and is not a movement of the body. Note the use of a bow in the following examples.

378a	b	c	d
Gesture, then rotate.	Gesture and rotate together	Use of third column	Leg gesture with chest rotation

Duration of a Rotation. A limb remains rotated until something follows to counteract it. This may be another rotation or a back to normal sign. Thus, a rotated limb will affect a following support.

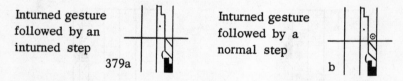

Inturned gesture followed by an inturned step

379a

Inturned gesture followed by a normal step

b

Use of Body Hold Sign. Where need be, a hold sign can be used as a reminder to retain a rotation. Although the rule is that any such rotation will hold until cancelled, the context of the movement often induces the reader to forget this and to negate the rotation automatically. In Fig. 380, the inward rotation for the right leg is held until the count of 4. This means that all steps and gestures of the right leg will be turned in up to that point.

As an added precaution, the rotation can be restated. However, such restatement should be introduced only where the writer has good reason to believe that without it the reader will make an error in movement.

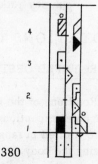

380

Types of Rotated Gestures. Rotations are only an addition to what is already stated in movement; they do not otherwise change the movement. Nor do they change any of the rules regarding touching leg gestures, jumps, and the like. Rotations do not necessarily hold you on the ground; the legs can rotate in the air as well as while supporting.

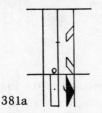
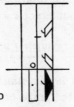
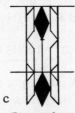

381a — The toe remains touching the floor during the rotations.

b — Toe repeats the touch; leg rotates.

c — Rotate legs during the jump.

Typical Examples of Rotated Leg Gestures.

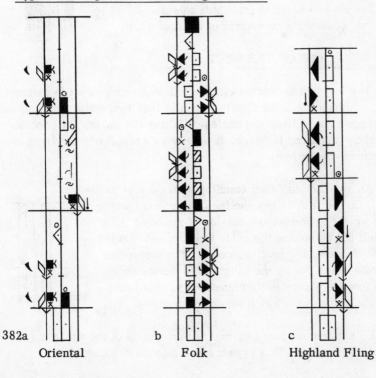

382a — Oriental

b — Folk

c — Highland Fling

ROTATIONS OF THE KNEES

Rotations of the knees fall into the same
category as rotations of the elbows. The knees
do not actually rotate, but a rotary movement
is achieved through the flexibility in the upper
and lower leg. Outward knee rotations are often
used as an exercise to counteract knock-knees.   383

ROTATIONS OF THE LOWER LEG

A rotation of the lower leg is similar to a rotation of the lower
arm but with a more limited range of movement. To understand
the action, sit on a chair with the heel of the
foot resting on the floor. Rotate the lower leg
in and out. There should be no action in the
hip joint; the movement occurs only from the
knee down. The rotation of the lower leg will
cause the foot to move from side to side. It   384
is not, however, a movement of the foot itself.

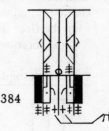

ROTATIONS OF THE FEET

The feet can be rotated either while supporting or while gesturing. Perhaps the most familiar form is that done while standing and
is known as "rolling the ankles." While the ankles do become
slightly displaced in space, it is only as a result of the rolling over
(rotation) of the foot.

As an example, start standing with the feet parallel. On the first count, the feet rotate out, causing
the weight to go onto the outside of the foot. As a
result the outside of the ankle is stretched. On the
second count, the reverse occurs. The feet rotate
inward which throws the weight onto the inside of
the foot (as occurs in flatfootedness) and it is the
inside of the ankle which becomes stretched.   385

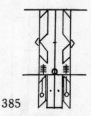

Do not confuse foot rotations with rotations of the whole leg
while supporting. This is discussed later in this chapter.

ROTATED SUPPORTS

Rotations During Steps. The leg can be rotated during the process of taking a step; that is, in the transference of weight. The rotation sign is then placed in the leg gesture column next to the direction symbol for the support.

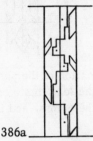

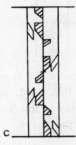

386a	b	c

Steps in middle level with legs rotated in or out

Steps in low level with legs rotated in or out

Steps in high level with legs rotated in or out

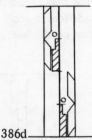

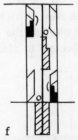

386d	e	f

Step rotated out; rotate in, swiveling on the ball of the foot.

Change level while swiveling. The "trucking" step.

Rotate both the supporting and the gesturing legs.

One of the most familiar examples of rotated supports is the Charleston.

387

"Charleston!"

Rotations with Weight on Both Feet. When the weight is on both feet, the legs can rotate in or out, either one at a time or together, the latter in either a parallel or a symmetrical manner.

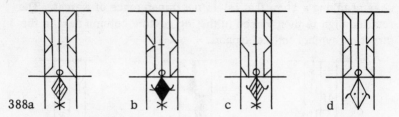

Because of the levels of the supports and the indication of the part of the foot used, it is obvious that in (a) and (b) the legs rotate on the balls of the feet, while in (c) they swivel on the points, and in (d) on the heels.

When the weight is on the whole foot, as in a middle or low support, the rotations cause a good deal of friction. It can be done, but it is rare. It is more usual to shift the weight slightly so that it is mainly on the ball of the foot or on the heel, and the rest of the foot is then free of friction. Since the spatial result is different according to whether the swivel is on the ball of the foot or on the heel, it is important to state which is being used.

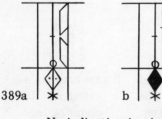 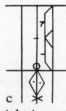 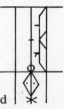

No indication is given of the use of the foot.

Weight is on the ball (heel just off the floor) then on the heel.

Weight is on the heel, then on the ball.

Most people will be familiar with the traveling sideways which results from symmetrical rotations alternating on the heel and the ball of the foot. There are many variations of this basic pattern. Sometimes the traveling is achieved through parallel rotations in which the weight is placed identically on both feet. These steps are used in Russian folk dances, as well as in Oriental and jazz.

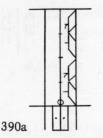
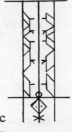

390a Opening into second position by means of rotations

b Traveling gradually to the right

c The same using parallel rotations

AMOUNT OF ROTATION

A relative amount of rotation can also be indicated when it provides a more suitable description. For this, the symbols × and ⌐ are used.

A very small rotation

391a

A small rotation

b

A large rotation

c

Note the difference in meaning when the qualifying symbols are placed inside the rotation sign and when they precede it.

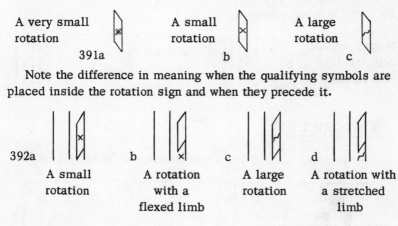

392a A small rotation

b A rotation with a flexed limb

c A large rotation

d A rotation with a stretched limb

An empty rotation sign means rotate as much as you wish. Degrees of rotation can be shown by using the black pins for 1/4, 1/2, 1/8, etc., in the same way that they are used in pivot turns. This amount of rotation is always relative - you have to know exactly where the starting position was. For this reason, it is often easier to describe the amount of rotations by where the feet (the front of the legs) face. To do this, we use the white pins which indicate the direction pictorially. They show outside direction as it relates to the body.

Legs rotated in 1/8

393a

Feet facing in

b

STATEMENT OF NORMAL

With most parts of the body there is a position which is obviously the normal carriage. Concerning the normal carriage of the legs, however, there have been noticeable differences of opinion. While some maintain that the feet should normally be held parallel, others insist that the average person employs a slight outward rotation in the legs so that the feet are placed at a slight angle. In view of the different structures of the body and the different environmental influences, Labanotation makes no final decision as to what is normal, but leaves each instance open for its own definition. At the beginning of each score, the meaning of the symbol normal can be stated in a key signature.

Normal means
with the legs
held parallel. $\odot$ =

394a

Normal means
with the legs
rotated outward
45 degrees. $\odot$ =

b

KEY SIGNATURES

The following illustrations show various uses of key signatures.

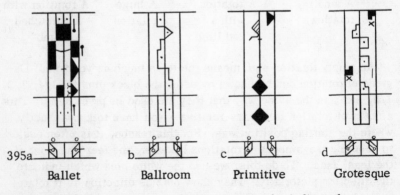

395a   Ballet   b   Ballroom   c   Primitive   d   Grotesque

Any departure from the key signature must be indicated.

CHAPTER XIV

Rotations of the Body

PROBLEMS OF ANALYSIS

Rotations of the parts of the body - the head, chest, pelvic girdle, and whole torso - bring up problems of analysis of direction which rotations of the limbs do not. To illustrate these problems, we start with movements of the head, since it is the most clear-cut in its actions.

The head rotates through the neck vertebrae, the axis for the rotations being an imaginary line extending through the top of the head. The head has a range to either side of about 3/8 of a turn. If a greater degree of rotation is to be achieved, it will require a slight participation of the upper body. In the examples below, the introduction of rotations does not bring up any question regarding spatial analysis.

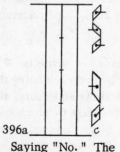

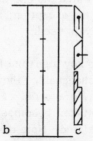

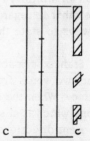

396a

Saying "No." The head rotates slightly from side to side.

b

The head tilts forward and then rotates while still in that direction.

c

The movement to place high does not cancel the previous rotation.

But in the following examples the notation description could result in two different actions, depending on the interpretation given.

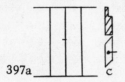

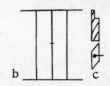

Rotate the head 1/4 and tilt it forward into the direction of the nose.

Rotate the head 1/4 and tilt it forward into the direction the rest of the body is facing.

Forward, here, can be interpreted as the direction into which the head is facing or as the direction into which the whole torso and the feet are facing, the original front. Both points of view are valid. To know which is being used, we introduce a key signature.

KEY SIGNATURE FOR "BODY" AND "STANCE" OR "SPACE"

The moment that twists occur in the body and a divided front is produced, the problems of orientation come up. Is direction for a movement to be determined by the new front for the part of the body that has moved or is direction to be determined according to the part that has remained stationary; that is, the original front? In describing movement both points of view are employed, the choice often resting on the motivation behind the movement pattern. Even in a single movement sequence there may be a switch between the one mode of direction analysis and the other. Rather than establish an arbitrary rule in which the one is considered the normal and the other is regarded as the exception, it has been found preferable always to state the analysis used.

Stance or Space. The key signature for Stance or Space is: ◆ . The two words are interchangeable, the idea behind each being the same. When the support, or stance, of the body is stationary, the front which it has established becomes the constant to which subsequent directions are related. Note that the black diamond relates to the white diamond used for a space hold. By using a space signature, we indicate that an outside front has been established, and this becomes a constant to which all movement descriptions are related.

Body. The key signature for Body is: ⊔⊔ . This symbol is a
very small version of the three-line staff which represents the body.
The use of this signature indicates a body constant analysis; that
is, all directions are related to the body: forward for the head is
where the nose is; forward for the arms is where the chest is facing;
forward for the legs and for steps is where the hips are facing, and
so on.

CHOICE OF SIGNATURE

The choice as to which signature to use rests with the writer.
The choice will be influenced by the type of movement. Extroverted
movement, in which there is an outside focus, be it the audience or
another performer, will demand a space signature. Introverted movement, in which the body is aware only of itself and is not related to
outside space, will require a body signature. The important thing
is that the reader be given an indication of how to view the movement.

PLACEMENT OF THE SIGNATURE

The signature is placed to the right of the staff, outside the
movement columns. When it pertains only to one part of the body,
it can be placed next to that part or, where need be, it can be used
as a pre-sign inside the particular body column which it describes.

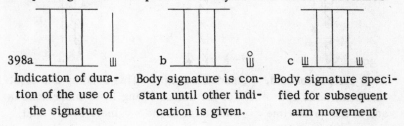

398a — Indication of duration of the use of
the signature

b — Body signature is constant until other indi-
cation is given.

c — Body signature speci-
fied for subsequent
arm movement

ROTATIONS OF THE SPECIFIC BODY PARTS

ROTATIONS OF THE HEAD

Following are various combinations of tilting and rotating the
head in which the key signatures have been introduced.

399a

The head rotates 1/8 to the diagonal and tilts forward (into that direction).

b

The head tilts forward and rotates at the same time. Since this is read from stance, the original forward direction will be maintained - the movement will be in a straight line.

399c

The head rotates 1/8 and tilts diagonally from stance, giving the same result as (a).

d

The head tilts forward and rotates at the same time; the line of the movement is a curve. Since this is read from body, the end result is the same as (a).

399e

After the tilt forward, the head turns 1/8 and at the same time moves diagonally from stance.

f

Another example of the use of stance for head directions.

g

This bending and twisting head movement is more easily read from body.

Note: If a body constant analysis is used when dealing with rotations, you do not get the same result in movement by bending first and then rotating as by rotating first and then bending. By using a space constant, a uniformity is achieved and this discrepancy is eliminated.

ROTATIONS OF THE CHEST

The third column on the right is used for movements of the chest and so a rotation placed in that column means a twisting of the chest. The chest twists or rotates from the waist in general principle, although the greater the rotation, the more of the lower spine is used. The chest normally faces front, and so any back to normal sign will mean a return to that state. In principle, the chest moves in a manner similar to that of the head, but it is more restricted. The arms are carried along during a chest rotation; that is, they move passively through space while maintaining their relation to the body. This is considered natural, and so this carriage of the arms through space is not written. However, if the arms should maintain their space relation in spite of the twist in the chest, a space hold must be indicated for them.

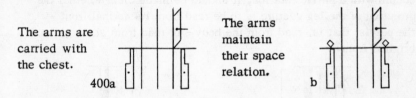

The arms are carried with the chest.

400a

The arms maintain their space relation.

b

A key signature was not needed here since the arms moved before the twist of the chest occurred.

When arm gestures occur at the same time or after a chest rotation, key signatures are needed for orientation. Following are examples of arm movements combined with chest rotations. Note the difference in movement resulting from the use of different key signatures.

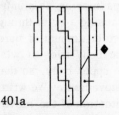

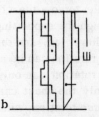

401a

After the chest twists, the arms lift into the direction of the steps.

b

The arms lift forward from the body, moving in the direction that the chest faces.

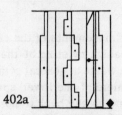

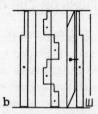

402a

As the chest twists, the arms
lift into the direction
of the steps.

b

The arms lift forward from the
chest while the legs walk
forward from the hips.

ROTATIONS OF THE PELVIC GIRDLE

The pelvic girdle rotates from the waist down and through the supporting leg or legs. It rotates as a unit. When a leg gesture occurs with a pelvic rotation, it should be made clear whether the direction of the leg gesture is to be read from its normal front - the pelvis; that is, read from the body - or read from stance, the original front.

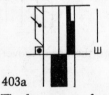

403a

The leg moves forward
from the hips.

b

The leg moves toward
the original front.

ROTATIONS OF THE WHOLE TORSO

The whole torso - the chest and the hips moving as a unit - rotates through the supporting leg or legs, causing a twist through the ankle, lower leg, and thigh. Only a certain amount of pure whole torso rotation can be achieved. As the body tries to twist farther, the rotation can only continue in the upper body, so that, in effect, only the chest can continue the movement. We write this as a torso rotation, since that is the intention of the movement. A chest movement per se would have a different motivation and expression. The term "blind turns" is given to rotations of the whole torso which are similar in result to pivot turns. Note Fig. 404.

A whole torso rotation is like
a regular pivot turn but with a
space hold for the foot.

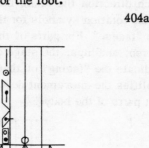

404a   or   b

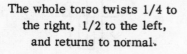

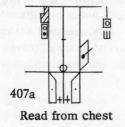

405a

The whole torso twists 1/4 to
the right, 1/2 to the left,
and returns to normal.

The torso twists while walking on a straight forward
path in space.

SPECIFIC "BODY" KEY SIGNATURE

In the exercise at the right, the question
arises as to whether the tilt should be into
the direction that the chest is facing or in
the direction of the hips, the supports. It
is very common in doing this exercise to
speak of forward as being forward from the
chest. Yet the whole torso bends from the
hips and logically should take its direction

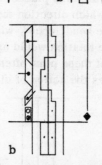

406

from there. To solve this type of problem, the body signature is
modified to specify "from the chest." Note the use of this in Fig.
(a) below and also note the use of the space key signature when
the direction is to be taken from the stance, the support, Fig. (b).

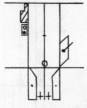

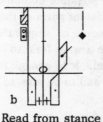

407a

Read from chest

b

Read from stance

USE OF STAGE DIRECTION INDICATORS

As a rule the stage direction pins are placed outside the staff on the left to indicate into which direction the whole body is facing. They are also placed inside the rotation symbols for limbs to show into which direction the limb "faces." For parts of the body such as the head, chest, whole torso, and hips, the stage direction pin in the rotation would also indicate the "facing" of that part. The use of these pins often simplifies the movement description and unifies the action of different parts of the body.

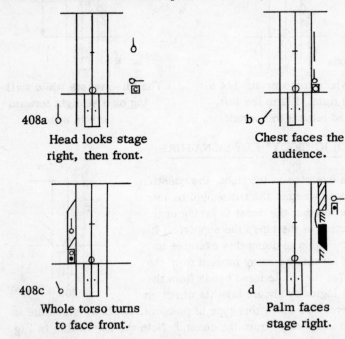

408a   Head looks stage right, then front.

b   Chest faces the audience.

408c   Whole torso turns to face front.

d   Palm faces stage right.

No attempt has been made here to go into full detail concerning all the possible combinations in the use of rotations and tilting by the different parts of the body. The possibilities of simultaneous movement, of sequential activities, and of interrelated actions provide a wide field to be explored in advanced study of movement notation. It is enough for now to understand the individual movements and to be able to put them to use.

CHAPTER XV

Revolutions of the Body

TYPES OF BODY REVOLUTIONS

The body can revolve in space in three basically different ways. In the terminology of the dancer or acrobat, since he is the one who most frequently employs these different forms, the three ways are:

1. Pivoting (turning) as explored in Chapter VI.
2. Somersaulting.
3. Cartwheeling.

ANALYSIS OF REVOLUTIONS: SPACE OR BODY CONSTANT?

When taken in their simplest form, with the body in its usual vertical standing position, the different forms of revolutions are not so hard to understand. It is when the body changes its relation to space that problems of analysis arise. The question also comes up as to whether complex forms should be viewed from a "body constant" or a "space constant" point of view. There are times for each; there is no hard and fast rule. However, certain usages have been found to be more practical than others.

Each of these revolutions has the possibility of two directions. In the following diagrams these basic movements are drawn next to the symbols which describe them. In presenting this material we wish first to make the use of the symbols clear. Details on how particular patterns are written will be explored later. Since any revolution is like that of a wheel around an axis, a wheel has been used in the diagrams for clarification.

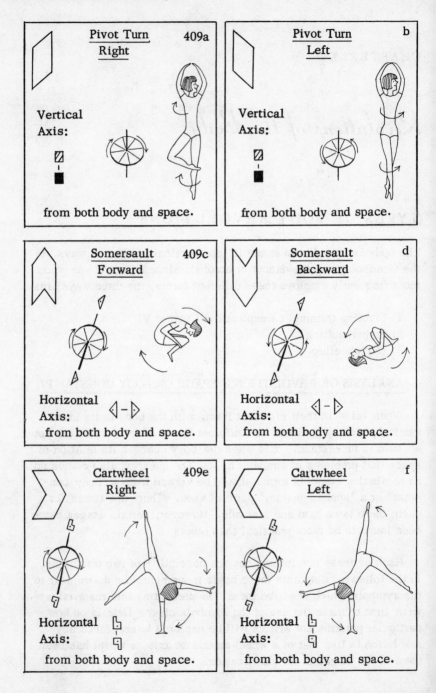

Pivot Turn Right — 409a

Vertical Axis:

from both body and space.

Pivot Turn Left — b

Vertical Axis:

from both body and space.

Somersault Forward — 409c

Horizontal Axis:

from both body and space.

Somersault Backward — d

Horizontal Axis:

from both body and space.

Cartwheel Right — 409e

Horizontal Axis:

from both body and space.

Cartwheel Left — f

Horizontal Axis:

from both body and space.

Before going into the actual use of the symbols it is helpful to see how these problems have been solved in other fields - ships and airplanes, for example.

It may seem odd at first to consider the motions of ships but the problems are surprisingly similar. A ship in the sea is like a person lying prone on the floor. The airplane is another vessel in a similar situation.

410

The different rotary motions are:

For a ship:	For an airplane:	For a dancer:
1. to yaw	1. to veer right or left	1. to pivot
2. to pitch	2. to loop the loop	2. to somersault
3. to roll	3. to bank (roll)	3. to cartwheel

The ship is more limited than the airplane in its movements since it rests on the sea. In the same way we are more restricted when we use the floor than when performing acrobatics or when diving both of which provide more spatial freedom.

The motions of the airplane are judged from the construction of the plane and not from its relation to space. In other words, it has a "body constant" signature all the time and the pilot's instructions are written in relation to the plane and his position in it rather than to the constant up and down produced by gravity. To make the plane perform a backward somersault, the pilot pulls the stick toward himself. From a normal flying position the result is a backward loop. If the pilot were flying with the left wing down (on his side), this same action would make the plane go around in a circle to his left.

411a

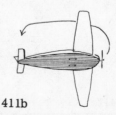

411b

LYING ON THE FRONT

Space Constant.

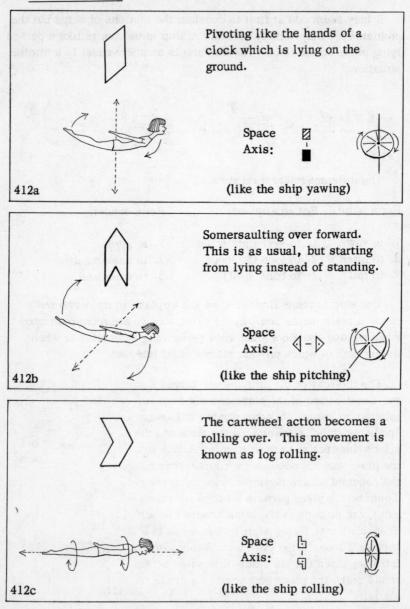

Pivoting like the hands of a clock which is lying on the ground.

Space
Axis:

412a

(like the ship yawing)

Somersaulting over forward. This is as usual, but starting from lying instead of standing.

Space
Axis:

412b

(like the ship pitching)

The cartwheel action becomes a rolling over. This movement is known as log rolling.

Space
Axis:

412c

(like the ship rolling)

Body Constant.

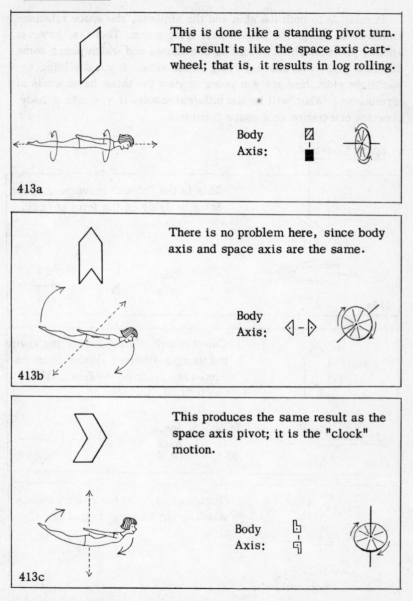

This is done like a standing pivot turn. The result is like the space axis cartwheel; that is, it results in log rolling.

Body
Axis:

413a

There is no problem here, since body axis and space axis are the same.

Body
Axis:

413b

This produces the same result as the space axis pivot; it is the "clock" motion.

Body
Axis:

413c

All these examples can be done in the reverse direction. Similar results will also be produced when lying on the back.

LYING ON THE SIDE

In relation to both the ship and the airplane, the space relationship was as though the person were lying prone. There is, however, another position which should be considered and which poses some different problems; that is, lying on the side. If you are lying on your right side, how are you going to view the three basic kinds of revolutions? What will be the different results if you take a body constant orientation or a space constant?

Space Constant.

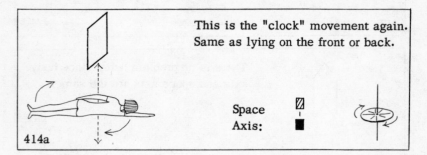

This is the "clock" movement again. Same as lying on the front or back.

Space Axis:

414a

Can this be? It's the log rolling again but using a different symbol from that used when lying on the front. Yes, theoretically correct.

Space Axis: ◁ - ▷

414b

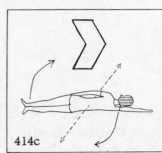

Cartwheeling, just the same as when standing but starting 1/4 of the way along.

Space Axis:

414c

Body Constant.

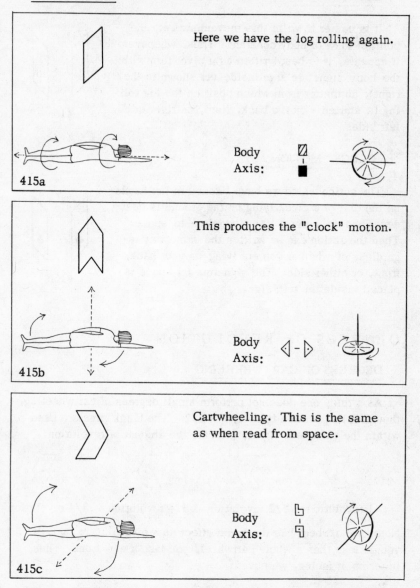

Here we have the log rolling again.

Body Axis:

415a

This produces the "clock" motion.

Body Axis:

415b

Cartwheeling. This is the same as when read from space.

Body Axis:

415c

If you compare the various examples shown on the previous pages you will see that certain motions are more constant when read from space and others are more constant when read from body.

LOG ROLLING

It is easier to write this movement from the point of view of body constant. Thus, whenever it appears, it is best written as a pivot turn with the body signature sign inside (as shown to the right), no matter from which position the log rolling is started - on the back, front, or right or left sides.

416a

"CLOCK" MOTION

The action which we have likened to the hands on the dial of a clock lying on the ground is best described as a pivot turn according to space. Then the action can be written the same way regardless of whether you are lying on your back, front, or either side. The signature for space is placed inside the turn sign.

416b

DEGREES OF REVOLUTION

DEGREES OF CARTWHEELING

As a rule, one does not perform small degrees of cartwheeling, though it is possible to do 1/4 or 1/2. The black pins are used within the cartwheel sign to indicate the amount of revolution.

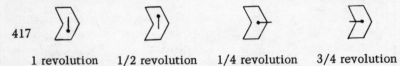

417

1 revolution   1/2 revolution   1/4 revolution   3/4 revolution

Note: A cartwheel has the same effect as a pivot turn in that, if you do less than a whole cartwheel, you face a new front. Thus, in terms of facing, we have:

418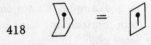

A cartwheel can be likened to revolving on a straight path.

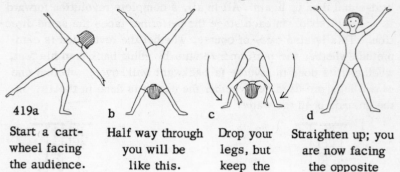

419a	b	c	d
Start a cart-wheel facing the audience.	Half way through you will be like this.	Drop your legs, but keep the body down.	Straighten up; you are now facing the opposite direction.

DEGREES OF SOMERSAULTING

Somersaulting is on a forward-back plane; no lateral movement is involved. Therefore, the black pins used for pivot turns and degrees of cartwheeling are not automatically usable for somersaults. A complete revolution is easily shown by the forward black pin. There will also be no doubt about the backward pin, meaning a half revolution. However, for the in-between degrees, 1/4, 3/4, etc., which occur more rarely, the fractions should be used.

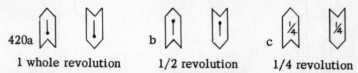

420a   1 whole revolution   b   1/2 revolution   c   1/4 revolution

No matter how much of a somersault is done, you will end up facing the same direction on stage. In Chapter XII we analyzed the directions into which you face when the normal up-down relation to space is changed. Here is an example to illustrate this point. Remember: a hand stand and a walk-over are the same basic revolutions as a somersault.

421a

The preceding illustration shows a hand stand which goes into a bridge and then up again. All in all, a complete revolution forward is accomplished. In each stage the performer faces the same direction. This is also true, of course, whether the revolution is completed, whether the performer returns by going back onto his feet, whether it is done in reverse (a backward walk-over), whether one or two legs are used, or whether the action is done in the air, on the ground, or in the water.

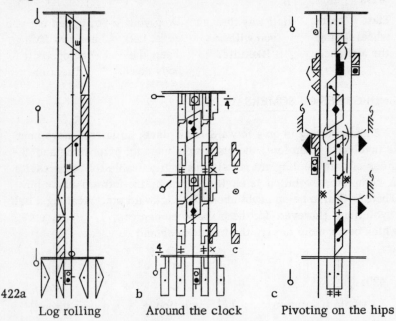

| 422a | b | c |
| Log rolling | Around the clock | Pivoting on the hips |

Note: Log rolling presupposes a space hold for the limbs.

REVOLUTIONS IN THE AIR

Simple revolutions in the air - that is, without special leg gestures - are written in the same way as simple pivot jumps. Two straight lines are written in the leg gesture column to show that the body is in the air.

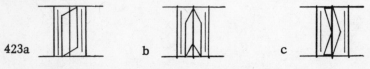

423a   b   c

In instances where leg gestures occur during revolutions on the ground, a hold sign is placed within the revolution sign to indicate that an aerial movement is not intended. In more detailed writing this would be evident from the use of the center of weight.

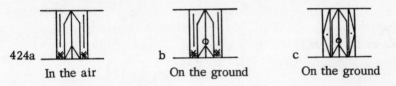

424a   b   c
In the air   On the ground   On the ground

In the acrobatic examples given below, no detail as to exact performance is given. It is taken for granted that you do not perform cartwheels unless you know how. The purpose of a score is not to teach such skills. However, in a book of instructions, notations on the correct use of timing, weight, and other factors must be given.

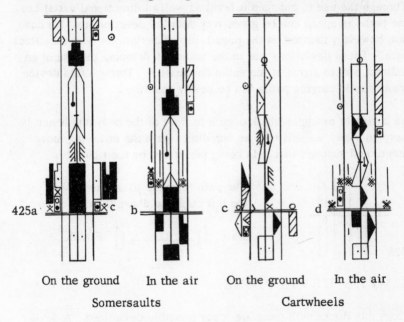

425a   b   c   d
On the ground   In the air   On the ground   In the air
Somersaults   Cartwheels

$\mathcal{D}$eviations

In describing movement, we speak in terms of the path in space of a particular part of the body. This path is the direct route between one point and another; that is, the starting place and the destination. Through the use of changes in level as well as directional variations, the paths in space can be given very detailed descriptions. We have not, however, touched on the possibility of deviations from the direct path. These deviations are in the nature of detours, the use of an indirect way to arrive at the same destination. Through this device many subtle curving paths can be easily described.

As a simple example which occurs in front of the body and hence is easy to view, we will take as our direct path the following movement, and suppose that it is being performed by the right arm.

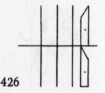

The path in space illustrated to the left could be drawn thus:

Start   ⬦———————▶ ⬦   Finish

426

SIMPLE DEVIATIONS

From this direct path there are many possible deviations. A deviation can be thought of as an outside influence, let us say like a magnet which pulls you off your path but is not strong enough to prevent you from reaching your ultimate destination. The possible outside influences for this direct path can be likened to an elongated sphere of which the path is the diameter.

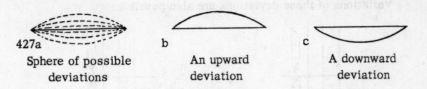

427a Sphere of possible deviations

b An upward deviation

c A downward deviation

A deviation can be into any direction and in any level from the established path. The important thing to remember is that the direction of the deviation is stated according to its relation to that line and not according to the directions as taken from the body.

INDICATIONS OF DEVIATION

The direction of a deviation is indicated by a small direction symbol. This symbol is small both in length and in width, being less than the width of the column. Because of its narrowness, it is easily distinguishable from full-fledged direction symbols. Every direction can be used for a deviation.

428

Note the difference in drawing the diagonal symbols, which are reduced to triangles.

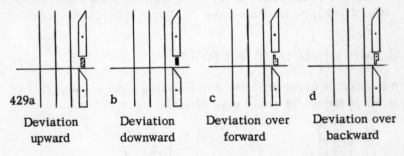

429a Deviation upward

b Deviation downward

c Deviation over forward

d Deviation over backward

In Fig. (c) the deviation over forward means that the limb must extend slightly in order to achieve this detour in the path. In Fig. (d) the limb flexes slightly in order to deviate backward from the path. Since the flexing is necessary to perform the movement, it is not written. In effect, this backward deviation means a path closer to the center of the body, but it is not described from this point of view.

Variations of these deviations are also possible:

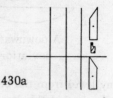

430a

Forward and upward
deviation

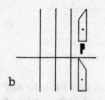

b

Backward and downward
deviation

ASYMMETRICAL DEVIATIONS

The outside point of influence will determine whether a deviation produces a smooth balanced curve or an asymmetrical, lopsided curve. Note the results of the following.

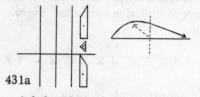

431a

A left side high deviation (as
judged from the center of the
line of path) produces this curve.

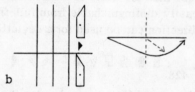

b

A right side low deviation
(judged from the center of the
line of path) produces this.

COMPOUND DEVIATIONS

It is possible to deviate more than once on a straight path. This is shown by the use of two or more deviation signs.

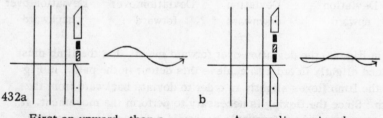

432a

First an upward, then a
downward deviation occurs.

b

A wavy line going down,
up, and down denotes
three deviations.

DETAILS OF WRITING DEVIATIONS

TIMING OF DEVIATIONS

The deviation symbol is regarded as a pre-sign because it is counted in the time value of the main movement. It does not by itself indicate the timing of the motion or influence.

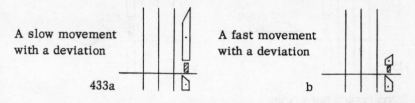

A slow movement
with a deviation

433a

A fast movement
with a deviation

b

The same holds true where there are compound (multiple) deviations: the main direction symbol gives the timing of the movement.

DEGREE OF DEVIATION

An outside direction can be shown to have a greater or lesser influence. The greater the influence, the more the moving part is drawn off its path. Conversely, the smaller the influence, the less deviation and hence the shallower the curve.

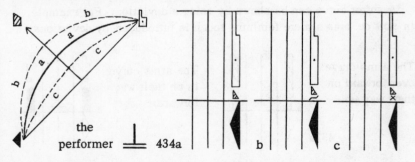

the
performer   434a

b

c

In the movement from side to forward, as shown in Fig. 434, the influence of the high diagonal causes a curve. Line "a" is the normal or average line of deviation. Line "b" shows a wide, or greater, influence, and line "c" a narrow, or lesser, influence. Note that a movement wider than "b" would actually reach into the diagonal high direction, thus becoming a full movement and not a mere deviation.

USE OF PLACE MIDDLE

The direction symbol for place middle represents the path itself. Thus, when this direction symbol appears after another deviation, it means an immediate, rather than a gradual, return to the direct path.

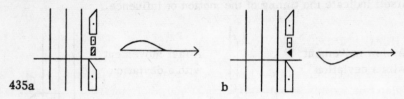

435a   b

TO DESCRIBE LOOPS

The basic movement here is one to forward middle. As the arm starts on its path, it deviates over the forward and backward diagonals in a clockwise manner; this produces a loop traveling into the main direction.

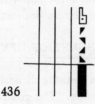

436

CURVES IN ARM MOVEMENTS

A softer curve can be shown by using a deviation. For example, in port de bras a more feminine touch is introduced by deviations.

The arms curve over forward on their way up.

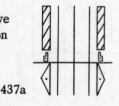

437a

The arms curve in on their way forward.

b

LEG CIRCLES; RONDS DE JAMBE EN L'AIR

Leg gestures also employ deviations, which are often used as embellishments. One form in particular, which is a fundamental exercise given at the barre in ballet technique, is the rond de jambe en l'air, a movement in space of the lower leg, the thigh remaining where it is and the action being confined to the knee.

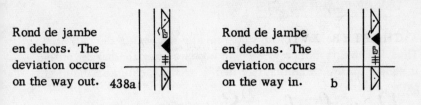

Rond de jambe
en dehors. The
deviation occurs
on the way out. 438a

Rond de jambe
en dedans. The
deviation occurs
on the way in. b

HEAD AND BODY MOVEMENTS

Subtle movements of the head can be shown by deviations. This
is also true for movements of the chest and whole torso.

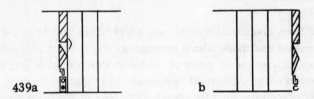

Remember: Interpret the deviation according to the line of the
movement and not in relation to the regular body direction. Thus, ℔
is forward horizontal from the center of that path.

CHAPTER XVII

Part Leading, Successions

PART LEADING

In Chapter X we discussed subordinate movements that follow the
main movement and those which accompany the main movement.
We now explore the use of parts of the body which lead or guide
various movements. A vertical bow is used to indicate leading. In
this bow is placed the sign for the specific part of the body which
leads or guides.

440a)   b)   c)   d)

Led by the hand   Led by the elbow   Led by knee   Led by hip

The difference between writing an inclusion and writing a guidance
must be clearly observed. In a guidance the indication for the part
of the body is surrounded by the vertical bow. In an inclusion the
vertical bow is broken and the specified part of the body is placed
within the break.

Led by the hip; the
hip motivates the   +)
movement.   441a

Hip is included; that
is, it accompanies   +)   +)
the movement.   b

TIMING OF A GUIDANCE

The vertical guidance bow is considered as a passing state; that
is, its influence lasts only as long as the bow.

The arm is guided upward by the wrist. At the
end of the movement the arm is back to its normal state; that is, the wrist is not flexed, and the
hand is merely an extension of the whole arm, as
is normal.

442a

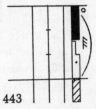

By the placement of the guidance bow, variations in timing can
be indicated.

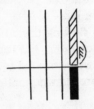

442b

The arm gesture starts with a wrist
guidance, but soon continues as
a normal arm movement.

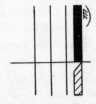

c

The wrist guidance occurs
only toward the end of
the arm gesture.

RETAINING A GUIDANCE

The particular position resulting from a guidance can be retained even though the guidance is
completed. This is indicated by a hold sign. It
is important to remember that unless a hold sign
is used a return to normal is always understood.

443

SUCCESSIONS, SEQUENTIAL MOVEMENT

The form of movement known as succession or sequential movement is one in which a movement flows from one part of the body
to another, passing from joint to joint. Perhaps the most familiar
example is the use of the arms in oriental dance. Here the movement is very fluid; a ripple can be seen to start in the shoulder and
pass sequentially through the elbow, the wrist, and the hand,
finally disappearing off the end of the finger tips. Similar waves
also pass through the torso, each vertebra in the spine being used
in succession.

SUCCESSIONS IN THE ARMS

A succession in the arms could be written
as a series of guidances, as in Fig. 444, but,
although it would produce the right result, it is
a rather cumbersome way to write the movement. A succession is a basic type of movement and so a special symbol should be used
for it: $\vee$. This represents an outward flow of
movement from the center of the body to the extremities. Occasionally an inward flow is indi-

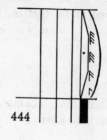

444

cated by inverting the symbol: $\wedge$. This flowing inward of a movement toward the center of the body is much rarer, but it does appear
occasionally. Note that these symbols, while related to those used
to indicate increasing and decreasing, are drawn smaller and are
placed within the column.

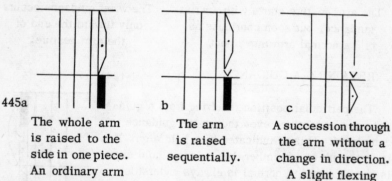

445a	b	c
The whole arm is raised to the side in one piece. An ordinary arm movement.	The arm is raised sequentially.	A succession through the arm without a change in direction. A slight flexing is understood.

Note the placement of the $\vee$ in the arm column. It is used as
a pre-sign when there is a change in direction or as a movement
sign (followed by a duration line to indicate timing) when there is
no change in direction.

CENTRAL SUCCESSION

A succession in the arm, where the outflowing motion starts in
the shoulder, does not normally affect the body. However, if it
should start in the center of the body, a special indicator is made:
a dot placed within the symbol: $\dot\vee$.

Here is an arm succession in which the flow
originates in the body. The use of the body
is a passing state, a return to normal being
understood.

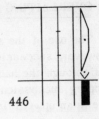

446

INWARD FLOW

The $\vee$ indicates an outward flow accompanying movements in
which the limbs open or are already extended. An inward flowing
sequence usually occurs with a closing movement of the limb, a
narrowing or flexing. The inward $\wedge$ symbol does not describe the
final position reached but rather the manner in which the movement
is performed.

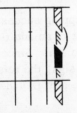

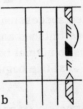

447a

b

The arm closes until it is across
the body. The upper and lower
arm move immediately into
their final destination.

The same final result but performed in a sequential way.
The part closest to the body
leads the drawing in.

ROTATED SUCCESSION

A succession can occur in conjunction with
a rotary movement. This will augment the action of the succession. In Fig. 448, the succession starts in the shoulder with an inward
rotation; as this flows out through the hand,
an outward rotation takes its place, gradually
working through the arm.

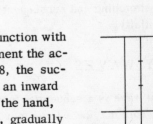

448

The arm successions in Oriental dance use only slight rotations
which are usually confined to the elbow.

OVERLAPPING SUCCESSIONS

The use of the symbol ∨ indicates one completed succession. However, successions often overlap; that is, before one has flowed out through the hand, another has started in the shoulder. Overlapping successions are usually in direct opposition spatially. If one is an upward flowing succession, the next is a downward flowing one.

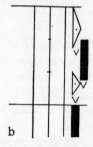

449a

Completed succession in the arm. Each one finishes and the arm returns to normal before the next one begins.

b

Overlapping successions. Note the use of an additional column for the arm. Since there is no pre-sign, the reference to the arm is understood.

SUCCESSION IN THE HANDS

Successions in the hands are also typical of Oriental dance as well as Hawaiian. Here the action starts in the wrist and flows through the joints of the fingers to the fingertips. A slight stretching and subsequent flexing occur sequentially.

450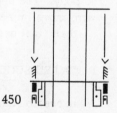

BODY WAVES

A body wave is a sequential movement which flows through the body. This may be a large movement in which the whole body flexes and stretches or a small movement more in the nature of a ripple occurring through the spine. It is important to point out here that technical dance training uses the body and space so specifically in certain forms of body waves that the sequence should be written in full detail to stress the exactness of performance. Here, however, it is sufficient to describe the sequential movements through the whole body in general terms, with the exact interpretation being left open to the individual.

This general form of description is especially desirable in teaching children as well as in ballets that contain character studies or dramatic sequences, where more detailed descriptions would hamper the freedom and spontaneity of the movement.

Here are some uses of the body in general descriptions:

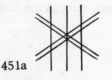

451a

The whole body is very small, closed in. This results in a crouch in which the limbs are close to the body and the head tucked in.

b

The whole body is very extended; spread out. This would result in the limbs being as open as possible. Exact performance is not stated.

Note, now, the differences in meaning in these examples:

452a

An outward development through the entire body

b

An outward development through the right side of the body

c

A development in the torso only

In these, no starting position or direction for the flow has been given. Note that when the development becomes more local - that is, in one part of the body or in one limb - the single $\vee$ is used.

The direction of the flow of movement is indicated by placing the direction symbols within the $\vee$. All such sequences start at the base of the spine.

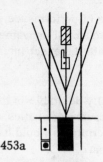

453a

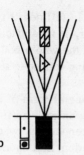

b

From a low starting position, a
succession goes through the body
over forward to up. The centered
direction symbols refer to the
wave, not to any supports.

From the same starting position a sideward succession
goes through the body.

IMPULSES

The term impulse is used for body waves in which there is a
strong dynamic start to the movement. The succession starts
quickly and usually peters out toward the end. This is also true of
the dynamics; the movement becomes weaker as the initial force is
spent. Accent signs are used to indicate the start of an impulse.

Fig. 454 shows an impulse upward starting on
the knees. In performing these movements,
exactness of performance is not desirable; it
is the sequential flow of the movement which
is important.

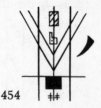

454

INWARD BODY WAVES

The inverted ∧ can be used for successions in the body which
result in closed positions. While these are not as common, they do
occur and should be understood.

From the high starting position, the body folds
up sequentially until it is in a low squatting
position. The action follows a backward and
downward path.

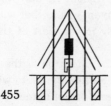

455

BODY RIPPLES

A small succession or ripple often appears in the torso. This is similar to a succession in a limb in that the part of the body does not move in space; there is only a slight stretching and flexing into the direction indicated. Where the movement is very slight, the deviation signs rather than the direction symbols can be used.

| A ripple through the torso over forward 456a | A torso ripple in a sideward direction b |

A duration line is used to indicate the timing. The sequence of movement in a wave through the torso starts in the base; that is, the hips. These move into the direction indicated, followed by the waist, the chest, the neck, and the head. As soon as the movement has passed on to the next part, each part returns to its normal place. The ripple has finished when the head finally comes to rest. Note the difference between the following:

| A body bend forward, performed in a sequential manner. 457a | A succession over forward through the body; the body remains upright. b |

CHAPTER XVIII

Details of Body Areas

STRETCHING AND FLEXING BODY AREAS

The symbols × and ⌐ can also be used for the body areas. The actions which these symbols represent may occur while the part of the body is in its normal position or while it is moving in space.

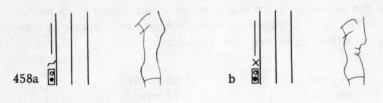

458a

b

The whole torso is stretched, pulled out.

The whole torso is flexed; the spine is rounded.

In these examples there was no change in the torso's direction in space, merely a change in the spine. In stretching, the torso pulls up from the hips and extends up as much as possible in space. In flexing there is a rounding through the spine. This is done so that the shoulders are still vertically over the hips. If the shoulders move away from the vertical, an inclination or tilt has occurred.

As we have seen in Chapter X, the torso rounds in the direction into which it tilts. In inclining forward, the rounding is over forward. In inclining to the side, the rounding is to that side, and so on. If a sideward tilt is accompanied by a rounding of the front of the torso, this must be written especially as an indication for the front of the torso.

THE TORSO

As noted in Chapter XI, we can indicate a particular part of the body through the placement of pins on the body area signs.

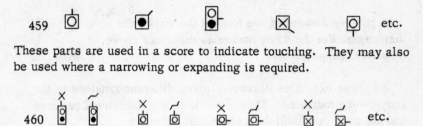

459   etc.

These parts are used in a score to indicate touching. They may also be used where a narrowing or expanding is required.

460   etc.

To achieve a flexing or a stretching, a slight displacement in space occurs. There is, however, no change in direction for the part of the body unless indicated.

TENSIONS IN THE BODY

Through the use of the above signs with direction symbols we can indicate a muscular rather than a spatial movement. This should not be confused with shifts in which the whole area is displaced.

The front of the chest pulls backward. This does not produce any spatial change for that part of the body but rather a tensing of the muscles in the front area of the chest, producing a feeling similar to holding one's breath in fear.   461a

The back of the chest pulls forward. Again, there is no displacement in space but only a feeling of tension between the shoulder blades as though you were aware of someone behind who might suddenly hit you.   461b

A pressing backward of the back of the pelvic girdle. Here the focus is on the vertebrae of the lower spine. Again, no displacement in space.   461c

A pulling in of the front of the pelvic girdle; that is, of the abdomen. In this case there is a spatial change due to the ability of the soft muscular wall to expand or contract.

461d

A pushing forward of the front of the waist, the diaphragm. For the same reason as that cited above, a spatial change occurs.

461e

As these examples illustrate, many different tensions in the body can be indicated. They often tie in with emotional patterns and are used in establishing characterizations.

PELVIC ROTATIONS ON A LATERAL AXIS

Chapter XIV described the lateral rotations of the pelvis, by which we mean rotations on a vertical up-down axis. Because of its construction, the pelvis can also rotate in a forward-back direction, on a side-to-side axis. This is the same form of rotation as a somersault. In this action the whole body revolves in space. When applied to the pelvis, the action is one of an isolated body area. While somersaults usually mean a full revolution, or at least a half revolution, the pelvis is limited in the amount of revolution it can perform.

DIRECTION OF ROTATION

A forward rotation for the pelvis produces a position known as sway back, or lordosis. A backward rotation produces the underslung or "debutante's slouch" position.

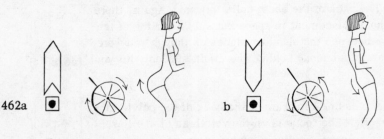

462a

Forward rotation   Backward rotation

The backward rotation is more easily performed with bent knees. It is, however, not necessary to flex the knees in order to execute it properly; this is largely a matter of habit and training. The forward or backward rotations of the pelvis can be done while standing, sitting, or lying.

The backward rotation in the pelvis is the basis of the contraction used in American contemporary dance. This is mentioned here so that dancers familiar with the use of contractions will readily recognize the means of recording it. The word contraction should be used with care since it is given different interpretations even among those who agree that the backward rotation of the pelvis is the start of the subsequent movement pattern.

DEGREE OF ROTATION

The degree of rotation possible in the pelvis is so small that it is best described in terms of $\times$ and $\curvearrowright$.

A return to normal carriage can be shown by the back to normal sign or by using the opposite rotation symbol with a back to normal sign inside.

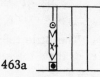

463a

A small backward rotation
followed by a return
to normal

b

A large forward rotation followed by
a backward rotation which carries
the pelvis to its normal position

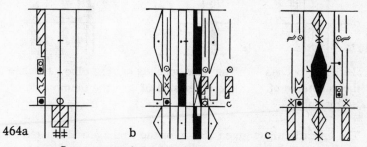

464a   b   c

Some examples using this pelvic rotation

DETAILS OF THE LIMBS

For purposes of touching or supporting it may be necessary to indicate a particular limb or part of a limb. To designate a limb, two small parallel lines are drawn above the joint sign which describes the action of that limb.

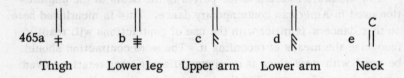

465a	b	c	d	e
Thigh	Lower leg	Upper arm	Lower arm	Neck

In each case it is the limb above the joint which is indicated, except in the case of the neck which is the limb below the head.

SPECIFIC PARTS OF A LIMB

Through the use of pins and of white and black circles, the different parts of a limb can be indicated. The same signs are used to indicate details of the hand and foot.

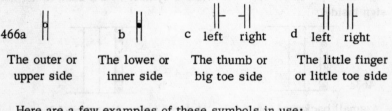

466a	b	c left right	d left right
The outer or upper side	The lower or inner side	The thumb or big toe side	The little finger or little toe side

Here are a few examples of these symbols in use:

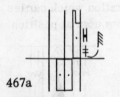
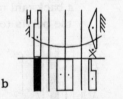
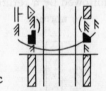

467a The hand touches the underside of the thigh.

b The hand touches the outer side of the upper arm.

c The elbow touches the thumb side of the lower arm.

The specific signs given above for the limbs are also used to indicate further detail for the hands and feet. (See glossary.)

CHAPTER XIX

Group Notation

The movements of groups and the changing of formations can be written in movement notation in addition to the indications on the stage plans. Only the most commonly met problems are discussed here; no attempt has been made to cover all the complex forms.

WHEELING

Unless a group of dancers is given instructions to circle as a group, each dancer in the group, reading his part in the dance score, will circle around himself. To indicate that the group moves as a body, the symbol ◙ is used. In this instance it refers to the center of the group. This means that the instructions are given for the person in the center and the rest must adjust accordingly in order to keep the group formation intact.

A group in a square formation walks forward four steps, then wheels half a circle to the right, keeping strict formation. The diagram to the right illustrates the notated example. Note that the symbol ↓ here means starting position and ▲ means ending position.

468

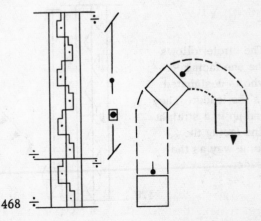

A straight line wheels
to the right 3/8 of a
circle, keeping the
line formation intact.
While steps in place
are indicated, in ac-
tual fact some danc-
ers will walk forward
and others back in
order to maintain the
straight line.

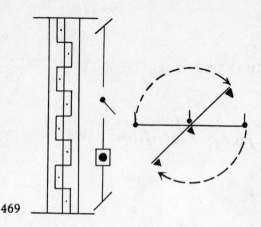

469

CHOICE OF A LEADER

Many dances contain "follow the leader" patterns in which the
performers adjust their patterns in order to follow the designated
leader. In the example below the dancers start in a circle facing
in. Normally, each dancer would take side steps according to his
individual direction in space. However, one dancer is designated
as the leader. His identity is indicated in a box placed on the right
of the staff. This designation can be made according to the direction into which the individual is facing, in this instance, ⟍ , hence
◹ . The identity may also be indicated by the letter given to the
dancer at the beginning of the score, as shown in Fig. 471.

The circle follows
the one facing ⟍
who is designated
as the leader. They
end up in a straight
line facing the
same way as the
leader.

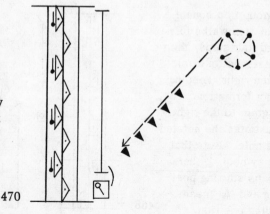

470

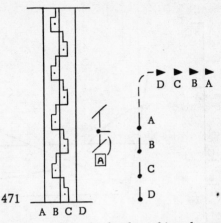

471

A is designated as the leader taking the quarter
turn to the right; the others follow in his path.

ENTRANCE AND EXIT STAFF

Entrance and exit staves are placed beside the notation staff on the right and
are employed when several people do
the same steps but enter on different
counts. The staff is a single vertical
line with short horizontal strokes on the
left to show entrance and on the right to
show exit.

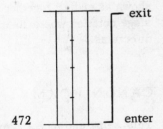

472

INDICATION OF PERFORMER

In most scores the individual performer is given either a letter or a
numeral for identification. This identification appears above the short horizontal stroke extending to the left of
the entrance and exit staff to indicate
when he enters or starts and below the
stroke at the right to indicate his exit
or when he stops.

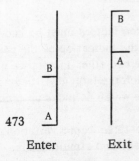

473

Enter   Exit

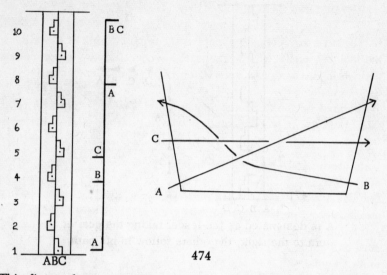

474

This figure shows a simple running pattern started by A. B enters on the count of 4 and C on the count of 5. A exits at the end of 7 and B and C exit together at the end of 10. Note that B and C are shown as ending together in the timing notation though not in the stage notation where their paths are indicated as being in opposite directions.

CANON FORM

This same entrance and exit staff is used for canon form. Many dances and ballets employ different types of canon form. It is a simple device familiar to both instrumental music and singing, as in rounds.

Three factors must be known in dealing with canon form. The first is the indication of the person or individual; this is no problem. The two other factors we must know are the count in the music on which the individual begins and the section of the movement pattern which he picks up (starts with).

The three basic varieties of canon form are: reverting, synchronized, and simultaneous.

REVERTING CANON

The reverting canon presents two common forms of movement: the isolated action which is repeated sequentially by the group and the continuous action pattern which is performed sequentially.

<u>Isolated Action Repeated Sequentially.</u> The most familiar form of this is the row of wooden soldiers who fall down one after the other.

In the figure to the right we have a simple lunge. Each dancer does only this one action, in turn, waiting in the previous position until his turn comes and holding the lunge until the canon staff has ended and all will again move in unison.

A starts the action on the first count, B does it on 2, C on 3, and D on 4.

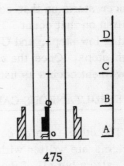

475

<u>Continuous Action.</u> This works fundamentally the same way as the above, but with the difference that the first dancer is given a continuous pattern of movement to perform. Each subsequent dancer starts the pattern from the beginning on the count designated and continues until the close of the canon line, at which point all join in the movement then indicated for the group.

In the notation to the right A performs the entire pattern. B starts on the second bar with forward hops followed by hops to the left. After these the canon line has closed and so B joins in the jumps in place. C starts on the third bar with forward hops and then joins in the jumps in place.

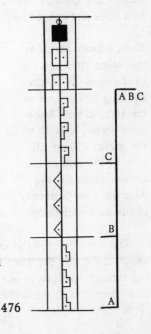

476

SYNCHRONIZED CANON

By synchronizing we mean that as each dancer joins in on a given count, he does what the others are doing on that count. Thus, the entrance line means not only to start on that beat but to perform the particular steps written on that beat.

By drawing a double horizontal entrance line on the left of the canon staff, we indicate that the dancer starts on that count to perform what is written on that count. Thus, B starts on count 3 taking low steps, and C starts on count 5 taking high steps. Once the canon staff ends, unison movement occurs as usual.

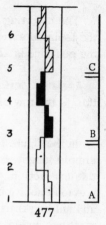

477

SIMULTANEOUS CANON

The other form of canon is one in which a series of movement patterns are written with each dancer starting at a different part of the pattern but all of them starting to move at the same time. Such canons are usually self-contained; they may be repeated but the action does not extend beyond the canon line.

Each dancer starts at the same time, on the first count. A starts walking forward, B to the left, C with backward steps, and D to the right. They all stop at the end of the canon, each having done all four patterns in his own sequence.

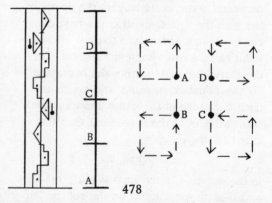

478

The logic behind the symbol for this form is that the start of the canon indicates the start in terms of time. The cross lines extending through the canon staff indicate that the dancer starts the pattern there and stops it there.

CHAPTER XX

Effort

EFFORT OBSERVATION

Effort observation concentrates on the manner in which a motion is performed. Similar gestures performed by two people of widely different temperaments will have different expressions because the inner motivation behind the gestures is different. In the same way a simple work pattern may be performed with different effort patterns depending on the mood of the individual at that moment. Behind each motion lies the inner originating impulse to which we give the name effort. Every action, from a tiny shiver to a jumping out of the way of an oncoming car, originates in some effort made by the individual. In daily life, we complete our various jobs and express ourselves in various ways through a series of effort patterns.

The use of efforts and the elements of which they are comprised have been studied, analyzed and recorded in work patterns of daily life, in industry, and in therapeutic work. The study of efforts can also be directly applied to the field of dance, where it fills the need for a specific description of the performance of a movement phrase.

The study of effort patterns in movement is one that requires detailed observation and analysis. A brief presentation is given here so that the reader may be aware of the existence of this material and so that reference can be made to its basic principles by those already familiar with this method of recording the various qualities in movement. No attempt is made, however, to acquaint the beginner with the full understanding necessary to the correct use of the symbols for efforts.

It is not the purpose of effort notation to convey the motivation behind movement, the intellectual idea or the emotional source. Such descriptions are conveyed more satisfactorily through words. Two different emotions may produce a similar effort pattern. For instance, a sudden increase in tension in the body to the point where motion is arrested may be the result of anger or of ecstasy. If it is important to know the underlying emotion, word notes to that effect should be included.

Most dance forms are built choreographically with the emphasis on the use of space and time. As a rule it is desirable to leave the finer details of performance open to interpretation by the artists. Therefore, in the development of a system of movement notation, the emphasis is on the spatial description of movement. Labanotation, as the first chapters indicated, records movement in terms of:

> The parts of the body that move.
>
> The direction and level of the movement.
>
> The timing, or rhythm, of the movement.
>
> The use of dynamics.

In describing movement in terms of effort, the first two items are relatively unimportant. The emphasis, rather, is on the area of dynamics. Effort is analyzed in the following terms: space, timing, exertion, flow (control).

Space can be direct (straight path) or flexible (curved path).

Timing can be quick (sudden) or slow (sustained).

Exertion can be strong or light.

Flow or control can be bound or free.

A brief description is given here of the use of these elements.

SPACE

For purposes of effort observation, the emphasis is on the use of space in terms of minimum use (a straight line) and maximum use (curves, deviations). It is not important whether a movement is in a forward direction or into a diagonal or side direction, nor is the use of level considered. The denial of, or indulgence in, space is the important thing, for this is what is revealing in terms of expression and motivation. The word "direct" is easily understood. The word "flexible" is the most suitable that has been found; it should be thought of as meaning able to change, willing to leave the direct path.

TIMING

The two extremes of timing - quick and slow - are familiar to all. In effort observation, timing is dealt with in a relative way. We are not concerned with exact tempo as set by a metronome nor with bars of music and the like. The concern is rather with the reason or need for sudden movements or slow, sustained movements.

EXERTION

By exertion we mean the amount of force or strength that is used, or the absence of this force. A resistance which produces a strong exertion may come from an outside source or may be produced in the body itself. The use of strength is easy to observe; the absence of strength produces a light, passive movement.

FLOW (CONTROL)

This is the least familiar element in the study and understanding of effort. No one word can fully describe what is meant and only a brief introduction can be given here.

Movement can be likened to a river whose course may flow rapidly or meander slowly. In spite of changes in its path and the obstacles which it may meet, it keeps flowing. It stops only when it meets an insurmountable obstacle or it merely peters out and ceases to exist.

Flow is the essence of movement. A free movement is one in which nothing occurs to hamper flow. A bound movement is one in which either the mover restrains the flow for physiological or emotional reasons or an outer influence exerts control and causes the movement to be bound. Even when a position is being maintained, it can be free or bound; this is understandable when you realize that a position is a movement which has come to rest or has been arrested. While there is a certain affinity between bound flow, strength, and slowness and between free flow, lightness, and quickness, these qualities are not necessarily inseparable: all of the different qualities of movement can be performed with either bound or free flow; there are no limitations.

THE EIGHT BASIC EFFORTS

By combining the basic elements described above, we find that there are eight basic efforts. For identification, each basic effort is given the name of a common movement with which it is closely associated. They are:

Space	Timing	Exertion	Name of Resultant Effort
Direct . . .	Quick . . .	Strong	- Punch
Direct . . .	Slow . . .	Strong	- Press
Direct . . .	Quick . . .	Light	- Dab
Direct . . .	Slow . . .	Light	- Glide
Flexible . .	Quick . . .	Strong	- Slash
Flexible . .	Slow . . .	Strong	- Wring
Flexible . .	Quick . . .	Light	- Flick
Flexible . .	Slow . . .	Light	- Float

Each of these efforts can be made using free flow or bound flow.

Some of them may not seem to have a place in dance and yet, when you are once familiar with the quality of movement they represent, you can readily see that, for instance, modern dance makes use of wringing motions in the body; tap employs flicking and dabbing actions; Oriental dance contains floating and gliding movements, to name a few of the most obvious.

The symbols used to represent the basic elements are as follows:

SPACE

The element of space is shown by a diagonal line; the direction into which it slants indicates:

479   /   \

  Direct   Flexible

EXERTION

The element of exertion is shown by the use of a single or of a double diagonal line:

480 //   \\   /   \

Strong, direct.   Strong, flexible.   Light, direct.   Light, flexible.

TIME

The element of time is shown by a horizontal stroke placed on the right or on the left of the diagonal line:

481 //-   \\-   /- etc.   -//   \\   -/ etc.

| Quick, strong, direct. | Quick, strong, flexible. | Quick, light, direct. | Slow, strong, direct. | Slow, strong, flexible. | Slow, light, direct. |

FLOW

The element of flow is shown by a horizontal stroke placed at the base of the diagonal line on the right or on the left:

482 //_   _   /_   _ etc.   _//   _\\   _/   _\ etc.

    Bound flow   Free flow

It will be noted that all positive elements - directness, quickness, strength, and bound flow - are placed on the right or slant to the right. The negative qualities are to the left.

EFFORT PATTERNS

To describe movement in terms of isolated basic efforts would be
like trying to talk in pidgin English. The observation of one effort
tells us very little; we must know what came before and what follows to understand the pattern fully. Thus it is the transitions
from one effort modification to another that are important. In effort
observation, a description might run as follows: "A sudden strong,
direct movement becoming increasingly light and flexible." Or, "A
slow movement, starting bound and becoming increasingly free."
Or, "From a light, quick, free beginning, the movement becomes
direct, then bound, and ends up free and increasingly sustained."
It should be noted that where one element is unimportant, or neutral, it is not mentioned in the effort description.

Effort observation and notation can be used completely separately
from movement notation or the two can be combined. When separate, a set of symbols different from those presented here is used.
They are more space-consuming, and so the smaller set described
in this chapter has been devised to fit into a dance score.

These symbols can be used outside the staff, on the right, where
the effort pertains to the whole movement, or can be placed within
the individual column when needed for that specific part of the body.
The effort symbols enrich the movement description. Often the
writer does not follow the complete movement pattern in his effort
description, though this is possible and is of particular value in exercises where the correct use of efforts is important.

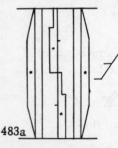

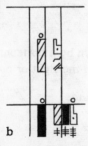

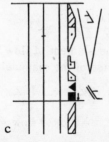

483a

b

c

| The movement is performed in a gliding manner. | A kick (punch) with the right leg | The arm starts with a slashing motion and becomes increasingly floating and free. |

Alphabet of Basic Symbols

Variations in the drawing of certain symbols as used by some European colleagues have been included in this alphabet in order to facilitate reading scores. These have been marked "alternate version."

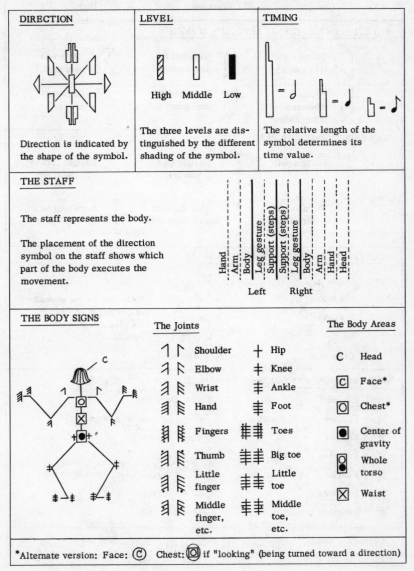

DIRECTION

Direction is indicated by the shape of the symbol.

LEVEL

High Middle Low

The three levels are distinguished by the different shading of the symbol.

TIMING

The relative length of the symbol determines its time value.

THE STAFF

The staff represents the body.

The placement of the direction symbol on the staff shows which part of the body executes the movement.

Hand | Arm | Body | Leg gesture | Support (steps) | Support (steps) | Leg gesture | Body | Arm | Hand | Head

Left   Right

THE BODY SIGNS

The Joints

Shoulder | Hip
Elbow | Knee
Wrist | Ankle
Hand | Foot
Fingers | Toes
Thumb | Big toe
Little finger | Little toe
Middle finger, etc. | Middle toe, etc.

The Body Areas

C — Head
C — Face*
O — Chest*
● — Center of gravity
— Whole torso
X — Waist

*Alternate version: Face: Ⓒ Chest: if "looking" (being turned toward a direction)

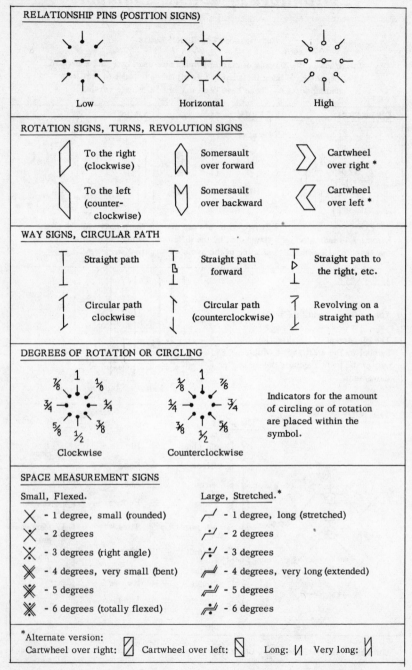

RELATIONSHIP PINS (POSITION SIGNS)

Low   Horizontal   High

ROTATION SIGNS, TURNS, REVOLUTION SIGNS

To the right (clockwise)

Somersault over forward

Cartwheel over right *

To the left (counter-clockwise)

Somersault over backward

Cartwheel over left *

WAY SIGNS, CIRCULAR PATH

Straight path

Straight path forward

Straight path to the right, etc.

Circular path clockwise

Circular path (counterclockwise)

Revolving on a straight path

DEGREES OF ROTATION OR CIRCLING

⅛ 1 ⅛
¾   ¼
⅝ ½ ⅜
Clockwise

⅛ 1 ⅛
¼   ¾
⅜ ½ ⅝
Counterclockwise

Indicators for the amount of circling or of rotation are placed within the symbol.

SPACE MEASUREMENT SIGNS

Small, Flexed.

- 1 degree, small (rounded)
- 2 degrees
- 3 degrees (right angle)
- 4 degrees, very small (bent)
- 5 degrees
- 6 degrees (totally flexed)

Large, Stretched.*

- 1 degree, long (stretched)
- 2 degrees
- 3 degrees
- 4 degrees, very long (extended)
- 5 degrees
- 6 degrees

*Alternate version:
Cartwheel over right: Cartwheel over left: Long: Very long:

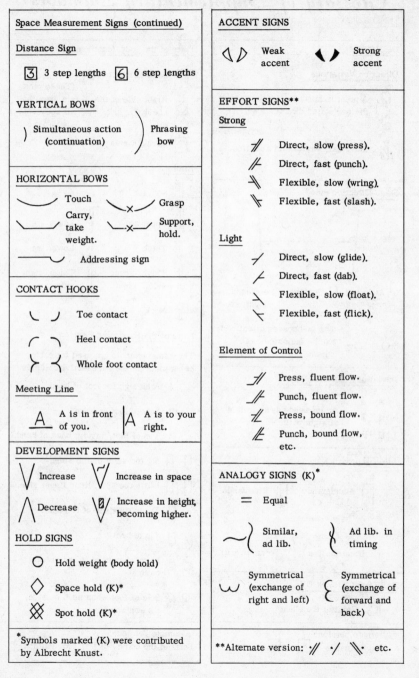

Space Measurement Signs (continued)

Distance Sign

⌐3⌐ 3 step lengths   ⌐6⌐ 6 step lengths

VERTICAL BOWS

) Simultaneous action
(continuation)

) Phrasing
bow

HORIZONTAL BOWS

⌣ Touch

⌣× Grasp

Carry, take weight.

×— Support, hold.

— ⌣ Addressing sign

CONTACT HOOKS

└ ⌐ Toe contact

⌐ ⌐ Heel contact

⊢ ⊣ Whole foot contact

Meeting Line

A̲ A is in front of you.

|A A is to your right.

DEVELOPMENT SIGNS

∨ Increase

∨ Increase in space

∧ Decrease

∨ Increase in height, becoming higher.

HOLD SIGNS

○ Hold weight (body hold)

◇ Space hold (K)*

✕ Spot hold (K)*

*Symbols marked (K) were contributed by Albrecht Knust.

ACCENT SIGNS

◁ ▷ Weak accent

◀ ▶ Strong accent

EFFORT SIGNS**

Strong

⫻ Direct, slow (press).

⫽ Direct, fast (punch).

⟍ Flexible, slow (wring).

⟍ Flexible, fast (slash).

Light

⁄ Direct, slow (glide).

⁄ Direct, fast (dab).

⟍ Flexible, slow (float).

⟍ Flexible, fast (flick).

Element of Control

⫽ Press, fluent flow.

⫽ Punch, fluent flow.

⫽ Press, bound flow.

⫽ Punch, bound flow, etc.

ANALOGY SIGNS (K)*

= Equal

~(Similar, ad lib.

{ Ad lib. in timing

⌣ Symmetrical (exchange of right and left)

{ Symmetrical (exchange of forward and back)

**Alternate version: ⫽ ·⁄ ⟍· etc.

Glossary of Supplementary Symbols

DIRECTION

Direction Variations

A point in space half way between the two stated directions

Move half way to this direction.

Stage Direction Pins *

Audience   Upstage   Stage right, etc.

The in-between directions can be indicated, as shown.

Deviations, Indirect Way

An influence away from a straight path

etc.

TIMING

Accelerando   Ritardando

Duration-line   Tremolo, trill.

PARTS OF THE BODY

Front of the chest*

*Alternate version:
Stage pins: etc.

Parts of the Body (continued)

Back of the chest*

Right side of the chest, * etc.

(These pins are used for all body area signs.)

Shoulder area

Limbs

Sign for limb

Upper arm   Lower arm

Thigh   Lower leg

Thigh, upper side.   Thigh, right side.

Neck

Parts of the Hands and Feet

The same symbols are used for each, being placed in their respective columns.

Area sign for foot or hand

Sole of foot or palm*

Top of foot, instep; back of hand.

Big toe side; thumb side.

Little toe side; little finger side.

Tip of toes; tip of fingers.

Tip of heel

Palm when used in the support column

Sole of foot when used outside its own column

*Alternate version:
Parts of the body: etc. Palm:

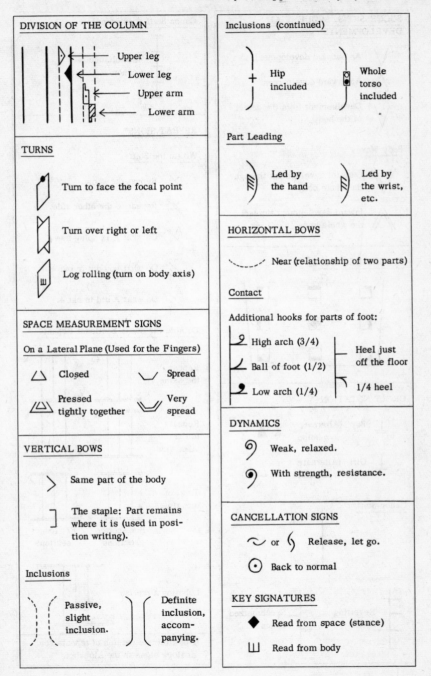

DIVISION OF THE COLUMN

Upper leg
Lower leg
Upper arm
Lower arm

TURNS

Turn to face the focal point

Turn over right or left

Log rolling (turn on body axis)

SPACE MEASUREMENT SIGNS

On a Lateral Plane (Used for the Fingers)

Closed   Spread

Pressed tightly together   Very spread

VERTICAL BOWS

Same part of the body

The staple: Part remains where it is (used in position writing).

Inclusions

Passive, slight inclusion.   Definite inclusion, accompanying.

Inclusions (continued)

Hip included   Whole torso included

Part Leading

Led by the hand   Led by the wrist, etc.

HORIZONTAL BOWS

Near (relationship of two parts)

Contact

Additional hooks for parts of foot:

High arch (3/4)   Heel just off the floor

Ball of foot (1/2)

Low arch (1/4)   1/4 heel

DYNAMICS

Weak, relaxed.

With strength, resistance.

CANCELLATION SIGNS

or   Release, let go.

Back to normal

KEY SIGNATURES

Read from space (stance)

Read from body

SUCCESSIONS, SEQUENTIAL DEVELOPMENTS

∨   An outward development

∧   An inward development

∨. Development from the center of the body

Body Waves

⋁   Outward development through the whole body

⋀   Inward development through the whole body

STAGE AREA SIGNS

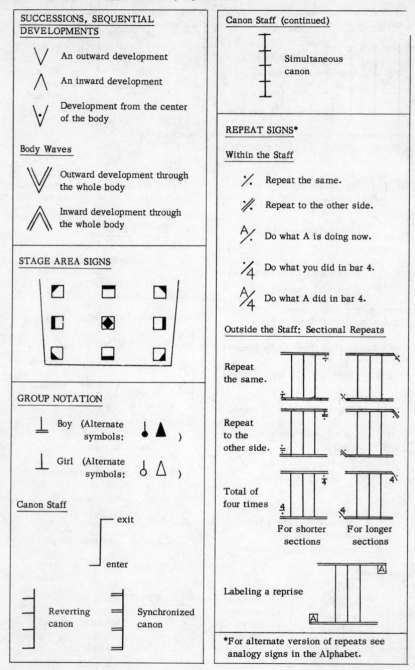

GROUP NOTATION

⊥ Boy (Alternate symbols: ● ▲)

⊥ Girl (Alternate symbols: ○ △)

Canon Staff

⌐ exit

⌐ enter

Reverting canon

Synchronized canon

Canon Staff (continued)

Simultaneous canon

REPEAT SIGNS*

Within the Staff

∕. Repeat the same.

∕∕. Repeat to the other side.

A∕. Do what A is doing now.

∕4 Do what you did in bar 4.

A∕4 Do what A did in bar 4.

Outside the Staff: Sectional Repeats

Repeat the same.

Repeat to the other side.

Total of four times

For shorter sections   For longer sections

Labeling a reprise

Ⓐ

*For alternate version of repeats see analogy signs in the Alphabet.

Index

Above, sign for, 173
Accelerando, 185
Accent signs, 120
Accompanying arm movement, 145
Active touch, 117
Addressing, 181
Ad lib., 88, 187
Aerial movements,
    occurrence of, 77
    writing convention, 52
Aerial steps, five basic
    forms, 54
Aerial turns, 91
Analogy signs, 186
Ankle, joints, 132, 134
    rolling of, 208
Arch, high, 124, 125
Arm-and-body movements, 50, 147-48
    study in, 59
Arm movements, 26
    backward, 50
    circular, 50
    crossing, 49
    curves in, 236
    direct path, 27
    flexing, 73,
        incorrect, 80
    level of, 16
    rhythms in, 38
    study in, with steps, 29
Arms,
    carriage of, 26, 33, 73
    column for, 12
    lower, movements
        of, 137
    parts of the, 136
    path in space, 27
    rotations of, 202
    upper, movements
        of, 136
"Around the clock," 230
Assemblé, 54
    incorrect writing of, 79
    turn, 91
    with brush, 122

Back to normal sign, 142

for pelvic rotations, 249
Backward arm gestures, 50
Ball of foot,
    support on, 124
    swiveling on, 209
    touching gestures, 120
    use in kneeling, 192
Ballet, arm position, 204
    key signature, 212
    positions of the feet,
        43, 55
    steps using brushes, 123
    steps, see individual
        names
    study, 143
Ballroom, analogy sign
    for, 189
    key signature, 212
Bars of music, marking
    off, 19
Battement, dégagé, 123
    grand, 123
    tendu, 123
Beat, breakdown of, 18
Beats, contact of legs in
    air, 70
Below, sign for, 173
Bending, see flexing or
    tilting
Blind turns, 218
Body, chart of parts and
    their movements, 152
    column for, 12
    hold, 92;
        for limbs, 140
    key signature, 214
    length (as a measure),
        161
    ripples, 245
    rotations, 213
    specific movements
        of, 151
    study, 159
    tensions, 247
    waves, 242, 244
Body-and-arm, see arm-
    and-body
Body areas, stretching and
    flexing, 246

Bound flow, 258-59, 261
Bow, for continuation, 189
    for inclusion, 149, 238
    for same-part-of-body,
        139
    for simultaneous move-
        ment, 138
Bows, use of, 138
Brushing leg gestures, 122
"Butterfly," 142

Cabriole, 70
Cancellation, hold sign, 63
    of previous position, 140
    of rotation, 203
Canon form, 254
    reverting, 255
    simultaneous, 256
    synchronized, 256
Carrying, 178, 180
Cartwheel, 222, 224-27
    in the air, 231
    degrees of, 228
Catch step, 61
Center line of body, 11
Center of gravity, 160
    analysis of distance, 161
    old version, 163
    situation of, 160
Central succession, 240
Charleston step, 209
Chassé, 123
Chest, facing, 156
    rotations, 217
    tilting, 155
Circles, of the arm, 27, 50
    of the hand, 205
    of the leg, 236
Circling, amount of, 82
    degrees of, 83
    direction of, 82
Circular path, 82
    situation of, 85
    size of, 84
    study, 87
Clock motion, revolving,
    224-28
Closed positions, stepping
    into, 169

Closing, the feet, 24
the fingers, 177
Columns, auxiliary floor, 200
division of, 142
use of, 12, 163-64
Contact, line for, 115
of the limbs on floor
while lying, 199
while sitting, 194
of the legs, 70
Contact signs, 178
Continuation bow, 189
Control, 258-59
Contraction, basis of, 249
Cossack jump, 135
Corps de ballet, 101
Count, breakdown of, 18
Coupé, 67
Crossing arm gesture, 49
Crossing step, 49
Curved path, 82;
straightened out, 93-94

Dab, 260
Dance drama, identification for, 102
Dancers, arrangement of on score, 105
Dancers' count, 19-20
Decrease sign, 174
Degrees of turn, 83, 88
in-between, 172
Details, recording of, 10
Development, see succession; increase
Deviations, 232
asymmetrical, 234
compound, 234
degrees of, 235
indicators for, 233
of head movements, 237
of torso movements, 237
simple, 232
timing of, 235
Direct (use of space in efforts), 258-61
Direct path, arm movements, 27
Direction, analysis of, 196
relative versus absolute, 79

symbols for, 13
variations, 171
Distance, of touches, 119
Distance sign, 182
Duration line, 74
Dynamics, 11, 183

Efforts, the eight basic, 260
Effort observation, 257
Effort patterns, 262
Élancé, 77
Elbow, rotation of, 204
Elbow joint, 132, 136
Elements of movement, 11
Ending, first and second, 112
Energy, see exertion, strength
in length of step, 48
Ensembles, identification for, 102
Entrance staff, 253
Entrances, on score, 107
Entrechat quatre, 70
Épaulement, 158
Equal sign, 186
Exertion, 258
indication in effort, 261
Exit, on score, 107
Exit staff, 253

Facing, 156
direction in room, 25
of the chest, 156
of the feet, 212
of the head, 156
of the palms, 33, 176
parts of body with use of stage pins, 220
Facing pins, 81
Fast, see timing
Feet, closed positions of, 43
closing the, 24
open positions of, 55-56
rotations, 208
Fingers, 176
First and second ending, 112
Flexing, choice of description, 144

of body areas, 246
six degrees of, 72
the arms, 73;
incorrect performance of, 80
the fingers, 177
the hands, 175
the legs, 71;
incorrect writing of, 80
the palms, 176
Flick, 260
Float, 260
Floor column, auxiliary, 200
Floor plans, 97-107
additional notes on, 114
placement of, 105
Floor work, specific symbols for, 200
Flow, bound, free, 258-59
(element of movement, 11)
indication in efforts, 261
inward, 241
outward, 239-40
Fluent transitions in touches, 118
Focal point for circle dances, 94
Follow the leader, 252
Following, arm-and-body movements, 145
Foot, key to parts of, 125
movements of, 135
rotation of, 208
sole of, 201
swiveling on ball of, 209
top of, 201;
use of in kneeling, 192
Formations, general for stage plans, 98
Forward-back symmetry, 188
Free flow, 258-59, 261

Gallop, 63
Gestures, see arm gestures, leg gestures
Glide, 260, 262
Glissade, 123
Grand battement, 123
Graph paper, use of, 17

Grasping, 178
Gravity, center of, 160
    force of, 196
Group action, general for
    stage plans, 99
Group or corps, identifica-
    tion, 101
Guidance, 238
    retaining a, 239
    timing of, 238

Hands, 175
    back of the, 176
    circles of the, 205
    column for, 12-13
    movements of, 205
    rotations of, 205
    successions in, 242
    waving the, 130
Hand stand, 162
Head, column for, 12-13
    deviations, 237
    facing, 156
    rotations of, 213, 215
    tilting, 153
Heel, hook for touching,
    115
    sliding gesture of, 121
    support on, 124
Height of jumps, 162
Highland Fling, 207
Hindu head motion, 157
Hip, movements of, 133
    supporting on, 193
Hold, space, for limbs, 141
    spot, 201
Hold sign, body, 92
    for the limbs, 140
    space, 92
    use of for rotations, 206
Hold weight sign, 52
    cancellation of, 63
    duration of, 63
    incorrect uses, 64
Holding, 178
Hooks, correct place-
    ment of, 129
    for touching leg ges-
    ture, 115
    qualifying supports, 124
Hop, 54
Hop, turn, 91

Hula step, 133

Identification, individ-
    ual, 101
Impulse, 244
In back of, 25
In-between degrees of
    turn, 172
In-between directions, 171
In-between stage direc-
    tions, 172
Inclusion bows, 149, 238
Increase sign, 174
Indirect way, see devia-
    tions
Industry, use of flow in, 11
"In front of," 25
Instep, use of in kneeling,
    192
Isolated movements of
    parts of the limbs,
    130-144

Jeté à coté, 123
    en avant, 123
Joint signs, 131
    choice of description,
    144
Jump turn, 91
Jumps, 54
    basic rule for, 53
    five basic forms, 54
    height of, 162
    level of, clarified, 61
    off the beat, 62
    on the beat, 62
    study in, 60
    traveling, 56
    types of, 53
    varied by leg gest-
    tures, 69
    with leg gestures, 68

Key signatures, 212
    body and space, 214-15
    placement of for body
    or space, 215
    specific "body", 219
Kick, 262
Knee gestures, 133
Kneeling, 190
Knees, rotations of, 208

taut, 72

Lateral symmetry, 188
Leader, choice of, 252
    follow the, 252
Leading, 238
    arm-and-body move-
    ments, 145
Leap, 54
Leap, hop, 62
Leap, turn, 91
Leaps, 51, 54
Legato, 39
Leg gestures, 66
    brushing, 122
    column for, 12
    during jumps, 68
    during steps, 67
    flexing, incorrect
    writing, 80
    level of, 16
    normal carriage, 71
    sliding, 121
    study in, 75
    timing of, 67
    touching, 115-123
    variations in, 69
Legs, circles of, 236
    parts of, 133
    rotations of, 205
    upper, 133
Length of step, determin-
    ing the, 47
    study in, 44
Length of symbol, 17
Length, statement of
    basic, 17
Level, 14
    changes of, 39-40
    of gestures, 16
    of jumps, clarified, 61
    of kneeling, 190
    of pivot turns, 89
    of support, 15
    of supports on the
    floor, 193
Lightness, quality of, 184
Limbs, contact with floor,
    194, 199
    details of, 250
    hold sign for, 140
Lines, use of in score, 19

Log rolling, 224-28
Long steps, 41
Looking, see facing
Lordosis, 248
Lower arm (limb), sign
  for, 250
  movements of, 137
  rotation of, 204
Lower leg (limb), sign
  for, 250
  movements of, 134
  placement in kneel-
    ing, 192
  rotation of, 208
Lying down, ways of, 195
Lying, space relation,
  197-99

Meeting, 181
Meter, 19
Metric indication, 18
Movement, elements of, 11
  nature of, 10
  versus position, 10
Music, effect on move-
  ment, 183
  marking off bars of, 19
  note values in, 17
  with dance score, 106

Narrow steps, 41
Natural movement, 9
Neck, 250
Normal, back to, 142
  statement of, 212
Numerals, use of in
  score, 19

Objects, use of, 179
Open positions, correct
  performance, 65
  stepping into, 58, 168
Opposition, 189

Palms, 176
  facing of, 33
Parallel arm movements,
  28, 186
Parallel rotations of sup-
  ports, 211
Part leading, 238
Partner work, 178

Partners' identification, 101
Parts of the body,
  specific, 131
Pas de Basque, 123
Pas de Bourrée, 123
Passive movements,
  145-47
Passive touch, 116
Path, circular, 82
  straight, revolving
    on, 93
Path in space, arms, 27
  description of, 10
  deviation from, 232
Peasant step, 42
Pelvic girdle,
  rotations of, 218
  on a lateral axis, 248
Pins, distinction be-
  tween, 96
  for degrees of circl-
    ing or turn, 83
  for floor plans, 100;
    written in score, 107
  for positions, 43
  relationship, 25, 173
  stage direction, 81
  use in columns, 220
Piqué, 77
Pivot turns, 88
  level of, 89
  on two feet, 90
Pivoting, 222, 224-27
Place, Where Is?, 20
Place middle,
  for gestures, 70
  use of in deviations, 236
Pointe, 124
Port de bras, 28
Positions, closed, of the
  feet, 43;
    stepping into, 169
  open, correct per-
    formance, 65;
    of the feet, 55-56
    stepping into, 168
Prance, a, 133
Pre-signs, use of, 41
Press, 260
Primitive key signature,
  212
Props, use of, 179

Punch, 260

Quality of movement, 47
Quick, see timing

Reading, notes on, 45
Relationship pins, 25, 43,
  173
  correct use, 48
Relaxed (dynamics), 184
Release, sign for, 120
Repeat signs,
  in the column, 110
  outside the staff, 111
  within the staff, 108
Repeats, sectional, 111
  with way signs, 112
Reprise sign, 113
Revolutions,
  degrees of, 228
  in the air, 230
  types of, 221
Revolving on a straight
  path, 93
Rhythms, even, 63
  in arm movements, 38
  steps in different, 36
  uneven, 63
Ripples, body, 245
Ritardando, 185
Rond de jambe, à terre, 123
  en l'air, 236
Rotations,
  amount of, 203, 211
  cancellation of, 203
  direction of, 203
  duration of, 206
  during successions, 241
  of leg gestures, 207
  of supports, 209
  of the arms, 202;
    lower arms, 204
  of the body, 213
  of the chest, 217
  of the elbows, 204
  of the feet, 208
  of the hands, 205
  of the head, 213, 215
  of the knees, 208
  of the legs, 205
    lower legs, 208
  of the pelvic girdle, 218

Rotations (continued)
  of the pelvis on a lateral
    axis, 248
  of the whole torso, 218
  symbol for, 202;
    placement of symbol,
    202, 206
  steps with, 31, 209
  traveling by means of, 211
  use of hold sign with, 206
  with weight on both feet,
    210
Run, a, 51

Same-part-of-body bow, 139
Score, arrangement of
    dancers on, 105
  coordination with stage
    plans, 103
  drafting the, 104, 114
  enlargement of, 113
  entrances, exits, 107
  music and dance com-
    bined on, 106
  placement of floor plans
    on, 105
Screwing and unscrewing, 204
Sectional repeats, 111
Sections, labeling of, 113
Sequence of action on stage
    plan, 103
Shaking, 185
Shift of weight, 167
  in kneeling, 192
  variations in, 170
Shifting, 157
  degree of, 157
Shorthand, notation not a, 9
Short steps, 41
Shoulder, movement of, 136
Shoulder area, 158
Side symbol, elongated, 39
Similar, 186-87
Simultaneous canon, 256
Simultaneous movement,
    bow for, 138
Sissonne, 54
Sissonne turn, 91
Sitting, 193
  ways of, 194
Skating, 125
Skip, a, 63, 133
Skirt, grasping a, 180

Skirt, grasping a, 180
Slash, 260
Slides, study using, 128
Sliding leg gestures, 121
Sliding steps, 124
Sliding supports, 124
Slip step, 63
Slow, see timing
Sole of foot, 201
Somersaults, 222, 224-27,
    231
  in the air, 231
  degrees of, 229
Space (element of move-
    ment), 11
  in support column, 62
  indication in efforts, 261
  key signature, 214
  relation to, 196;
    while lying, 198
  use of in efforts, 258-59
Space hold, 92, 141
Specific movements of the
    body, 151
Specific stage notation, 100
Spiral, circular path, 86
Spot hold, 201
Spreading the fingers, 177
Staccato, 39
  steps, 37, 52
Staff, the, 11
Stage area, description
    of, 97
  signs for specific, 182
Stage direction indicators,
    81, 172
  use in columns, 220
Stage plans, 97
  coordination of with
    score, 103
  general formations, 98
  general group action, 99
  general grouping, 98
  identification of dan-
    cers on, 101-2
  movement description
    on, 104
  sequence of action
    on, 103
  specific notation, 100
Stamps, 120
"Stance" key signature, 214

Staple, use of, 59
Steps, 23-25
  breakdown of, 30
  change of level
    during, 40
  clarification, 30
  crossing, performance
    of, 49
  indication of style, 42
  length of, 41
  performance of, 32
  rhythms in, 36-37
  rotation during, 209
  sliding, 125
  staccato, 37
Straightened-out-curved
    path, 93
Strength (dynamics), 184
Stretching, the arms, 73
  the body areas, 246
  the fingers, 177
  the hands, 175
  the legs, 71
  the palms, 176
Studies,
  body-and-arm, 159
  circular path, 87
  joints, 143
  jumps, 60
  length of steps, rhy-
    thms, 44
  leg gestures, 75
  steps and arm move-
    ments, 29
  slides and brushes, 128
  turns, 95
Successions, 239
  central, 240
  in the arms, 240
  in the hands, 242
  inward flow, 241
  overlapping, 242
  with rotation, 241
Sudden, indicated in
    efforts, 259
Support, absence of, 51
  column for, 12
  levels of, 15;
    variations in, 125-27
  on different parts of the
    foot, 124
  on the hips, 193

Support, (continued)
  on the knees, 190
  on the torso, 195
  qualified by hooks, 124
  rotated, 209
  sliding, 124
Supporting a partner, 178
Sustained steps, 37
Sustained movement,
  correct performance, 48
  indicated in efforts, 259
Sway back, 248
Swing, of the arms, 28, 183
  timing of a, 46
Swiveling on ball of foot,
  209
Symbols, absence of, 27
  placement of, 15
Symmetrical, 186, 188
Symmetrical arm move-
  ments, 28
Symmetrical repeat, 108
Synchronized canon, 256
Syncopation in jumps, 62

Taut knees, 72
Tempo, exact, 47
Tensions in the body, 247
Texture, affected by
  timing, 47
  of movement, 11
Thigh (limb) sign for, 250
  movements of, 133
Tilting, 153
  the chest, 155
  the head, 153
  the whole torso, 154
Time, indication in
  efforts, 261
Timing, accelerando,
  ritardando, 185
  ad lib., 187
  basic explanations, 17
  (element of move-
  ment), 11
  its effect on move-
  ment, 46
  of deviations, 235
  of touching gestures, 118
  of a guidance, 238
  sudden, sustained,
  258-59

Toe, hook for touching, 115
  sliding gesture, 121
  support on, 124
Torso, deviations of, 237
  flex and stretch, 154, 246
  whole, tilting, 154
Touches, active, 117
  consecutive, 118
  distance of, 119
  fluent transitions, 118
  passive, 116
  variations in, 119
Touching, greater details,
  174
Touching gestures, timing
  of, 118
Touching leg gestures, 70
Transference of weight, 30
Traveling, by means of
  rotations, 211
Traveling jumps, 56
  clarifications, 65
Tremolo, 185
Trill, 185
Triplet, 18
Trucking step, 209
Turn out, use of, 31
Turns, amount of, 88
  blind, 218
  direction of, 88
  clarifications, 96
  in the air, 91
  in-between degrees, 172
  on two feet, 90
  pivot, 88;
  levels of, 89
  study in, 95
Twist, see rotations

Upbeat, 18
  preparation, 46
Upper arm (limb) sign
  for, 250
  movements of, 136
Upper leg (limb) sign
  for, 250
  movements of, 133

Vibrating, 185

Walk, analysis of, 9
Walking on knees, 191

Waltz, basis of, 23
  step, 42
Waves, body, 242
  inward body, 244
Waving the hand, 130
Waving line, path of
  gesture, 234
Way signs, see also circular path
  clarifications, 64
  straight, 58
  use of repeats with, 112
Weak (dynamics), 184
Weight, hold, see hold
  weight
  shift of, 167;
  variations in, 170
  transference of, 30
Wheeling, 251
Where Is Place?, 20
Whole foot, hook for
  touching, 115
  sliding gestures, 121
  support on flat foot, 124
Whole torso, rotations
  of, 218
  tilting, 154
  shifting, 157
Wide steps, 41
Wring, 260